STORIES FROM MY JOURNEY

STORIES FROM MY JOURNEY

By the Reverend Arthur H. Holt

Advocate Press, Columbia, South Carolina

Copyright © 2025 by Advocate Press

Scripture quotations marked (NIV) are taken from The Holy Bible, New International Version, Copyright © 1973, 1978, 1984 by the International Bible Society. THE HOLY BIBLE, NEW INTERNATIONAL VERSION®, NIV® Copyright © 1973, 1978, 1984, 2011 by Biblica, Inc.® Used by permission. All rights reserved worldwide.

All rights reserved. No part of this book may be reproduced or transmitted in any form or by any means, electronic or mechanical, including photocopying, recording, or by any information storage and retrieval system, without permission in writing from the publisher.

First published in the United States of America in 2025

Library of Congress Cataloging-in-Publication Data
Stories from My Journey
p. cm.

ISBN 978-1-966237-08-2

This book is dedicated to Penny Holt, my wife of fifty-three years, and to our children, Hillary and John, who taught me most of what I know about God's unconditional love!

Table of Contents

Preface ix
Part 1: Stories from My Childhood
    Chapter 1: Mom and Dad 3
    Chapter 2: Penny 9
    Chapter 3: Doug Pridgeon 12
    Chapter 4: Mike Blanton 17
    Chapter 5: Whitney's Steve Cannon 21
    Chapter 6: The Backyard Gang 24
    Chapter 7: Mrs. Thompson and Her Mistletoe 27
    Chapter 8: Jimmy Bozard 29
Part 2: Mentors
    Chapter 9: Addendum to the Story about Doug Bowling ..35
    Chapter 10: Wes Voigt 37
    Chapter 11: Carl Clary and the College Place Youth 39
    Chapter 12: The Reverend John Rowland 43
    Chapter 13: The Reverend Joe Alley 48
    Chapter 14: The Reverend John Rush 52
Part 3: Stories about Church Members
    Chapter 15: Moose Teter 57
    Chapter 16: Odell and Mae Bledsoe 59
    Chapter 17: Mrs. Kate 64
    Chapter 18: Bob and Barbara Kay 67
    Chapter 19: Dinty Moore 70
    Chapter 20: John I. Warner Jr. 73
    Chapter 21: Memorable Baptisms 75
    Chapter 22: Bill Gibbons 77
    Chapter 23: Practical Jokesters 81
    Chapter 24: A Kidding Custodian 83
    Chapter 25: Find the Crazies.......................................85
Part 4: Things I Wrote for Facebook
    Chapter 26: I Know I Am a Little Different 91
    Chapter 27: Are You Watching Me, Jesus? 93
    Chapter 28: The God I Believe in Never Changes 94

Chapter 29: Diversity 95
Chapter 30: The United Methodist Church 96
Chapter 31: A Lesson from Acts 10 98
Chapter 32: My Simple Tract 101
Chapter 33: The Teacher 102
Chapter 34: It Takes No Talent 104
Chapter 35: Let's Go Back 106
Chapter 36: Disaffiliation 107
Conclusion...109
About the Author..113

Preface

I am as surprised as anyone that things I have written were deemed worthy of being printed in book form by the Advocate Press and its editor Jessica Brodie. The honest truth is that my stories would still be hidden away on this computer if it had not been for Jessica's encouragement.

As a "superannuated pastor," I miss the opportunities I once had to tell people the stories of Jesus and his present-day disciples. Thank you for reading these books, and I hope I sometimes inspire you and sometimes make you think about what you believe and how you have experienced God.

—Arthur H. Holt

Part 1
Stories from My Childhood

Chapter 1

Mom and Dad

Since this is the second book I have written about important stories and people of my journey, I can't let this chance pass to tell you a bit about my parents—although they deserve volumes and not just a few pages.

Let me begin by saying nobody has ever had better parents than my sister Caroline and I did. We stand on their shoulders just as surely as they stood on their parents' shoulders. As I write this, I am so keenly aware that I am not a self-made man, and I am so thankful for Hardin and Caroline Holt.

There was a dynamic in my home that had a profound effect on me. My parents came from two very different worlds that were separated by less than ten miles. Mama was from the city and had a college education, as did her ancestors several generations back. Daddy grew up on a farm and had finished the eleven grades of public education in just fifteen years (he always did want to get his money's worth). He dropped out several times, once telling his papa that he wanted to stay home with him and farm. But one summer of full-time farming led Daddy to give high school another chance.

Born in 1910, he was six years older than my mother, but thanks to his stellar school performance, they finished high school at about the same time.

The fact that my parents were from two very different worlds was obvious to all four of my grandparents. My sister expresses it this way: "Mama's parents weren't at all sure about their son-in-law. They thought their daughter had hitched her wagon to a lame horse. Meanwhile, Daddy's parents thought our mother was uppity and snooty because she wanted two sheets on her bed, and she plucked her eyebrows. They also criticized my mom for shaving her legs! In the opinion of the Holts, girls who did this were going to hell."

When we went to see my mother's parents (the Cannons), we went to their modern home with central heat and indoor plumbing. At Daddy's parents' home, which had been built soon after the turn of the twentieth century, there was a fireplace in every room, and there were several wasp-inhabited outhouses! Mama had grown up with a modern bathtub; Daddy's family had a portable round metal tub that had to have water heated on the kitchen stove and poured into it (and usually more than one child would use the same recycled water). Food served to me by my maternal grandmother was cooked on a modern electric stove and oven; Grandmother Holt never cooked on anything except an old wood stove. Since I was a product of these different worlds, I never knew whether I was Metropolitan Opera or the Grand Ole Opry.

My parents were also from different theological worlds, even though they were both raised in Methodist churches. Mama's faith was a product of Christian education. She was sure that teaching people the faith was the best way to spread the Good News. Mama was always calm and rational and emphasized the power of unconditional love. Daddy's faith experience was much more grounded in his emotions. He had responded to an altar call during a revival, and there was always a lot of fear and uncertainty in his faith. I often heard him say (and was somewhat embarrassed when he said it) that he needed help getting into heaven and that is why he had married Mom. These two faith traditions had a profound impact on my own spiritual journey. Part of me wanted emotional religious experiences and another part of me didn't trust those experiences, preferring a more rationally based faith. Perhaps that is why I trekked through Charismatic and Lutheran traditions on my way to the theological liberalism that guides my faith today.

Mom and Daddy started dating in the late 1930s. When the United States entered World War II, Dad was drafted at the age of thirty-two. Mom had a budding career as a schoolteacher at Drayton Elementary School and later as an employee of the Upper South Carolina Annual Conference of the Methodist Episcopal Church, South as a trainer of Sunday school teachers and the director of the Epworth League Methodist Student Center at Winthrop College. Therefore, discussions about their future together had not fully ripened when he went off to basic training at Camp Butner, North Carolina.

Daddy explained how it happened that he and Mama became engaged. One evening at Camp Butner, he and a buddy were walking back to the base when he was struck by a drunk driver and "knocked out of his shoes," landing in a ditch seventy-two feet from the accident. Mama was called to come see him quickly because he was not expected to live. But by the time she drove the distance to the camp—in her old car that Daddy called "Shasta" (because she-has-to be pushed to get her cranked)—Daddy had regained consciousness. He could have been honorably discharged right then, but he and his buddies were ready to go retake Europe from Hitler. But he did get a promise from Mama that she would marry him immediately when he got back home after the war.

World War II ended in the summer of 1945. Daddy got home from Europe in December 1945. They were married on January 18, 1946.

After their marriage, Mom and Dad lived out in the country in a rented house in the Liberty Church community where Daddy had grown up. The home was heated by a coal-fired potbellied stove. Early every morning, Daddy would go out to the shed in the backyard to get two large buckets of coal that Mom would use to keep the fire burning all day. Every day he would lift those two buckets just like he was supposed to, using his knees to lift the load while he kept his back straight. And to hear him tell it, every day as he straightened his knees, he would hit his head on an overhead rafter and have to put the buckets back down again until his head quit hurting. I suppose that if one is half asleep, cold, and working in the dark, it would be easy to repeat the same mistake day after day. After Daddy staggered back into the house with the buckets of coal, he would continue getting ready for work as Mom fixed their breakfast.

One day when his cranial crunch had been especially severe, Daddy could not find his new false teeth anywhere. They were not in their bowl. They weren't in a pocket. He turned the house upside down looking for his store-bought teeth without luck. This meant that he would have to go to work—and call on his customers—without his teeth, and that was an awful prospect for him. Daddy was very upset and mad about his missing teeth as he and Mama sat down to their breakfast together.

The first rays of sun were just coming up over the horizon and making their way into the dark shed when my parents looked out the kitchen window and saw something strange. It looked to them like something was glowing brightly from inside that shed. Whatever it was, it was in stark contrast to the black pile of coal that the object was perched on top of, and so Daddy went to investigate. It turned out that the brightly glowing object was his false teeth lying there on the coal! That morning, when he hit his head, he had not been knocked out, but apparently his teeth had been.

My mother was not happy living way out in the country. She especially didn't like always being cold because of the coal or have her babies living under the constant threat of a stove pipe explosion that once covered my sister in soot everywhere, though her lips were protected by her pacifier. Somehow Mama convinced Daddy to move into town into a radiator-heated apartment at Highland Court, which was located across the street from her great-grandparents' old home.

The move from the country to the city meant that Dad had to liquidate his stock, or rather, get rid of his chickens. No one wanted his last two hens, so he began asking around, trying to find them a home. Finally, a man offered to trade Dad two goats for the chickens, and he agreed.

Mom was not as excited about the hens-for-goats trade as my father was. She thought that the goats would not look good on a city lawn, plus the thought of her two children getting butted by goats didn't exactly thrill her. So Dad began to look again for a way to get rid of his goats. He found a jeweler who loved goat's milk who offered Dad a bunch of beautiful watches in trade for them.

To say the least, Dad was thrilled with his trades, so thrilled that he told everyone about them. One of the people who heard the story offered my father a used car in exchange for the watches. A few weeks later, when Daddy was repeating his fantastic story, another man wanted the old car and bought it from Dad for $150.

Now if my arithmetic is right, that means Daddy's two chickens were worth $75 a piece! That would be a great deal in today's economy, but imagine what $150 was worth in 1951. It was equal to two weeks' pay at least. My father had the gift of storytelling and the ability to sell almost anything, and when he used the talents he had been given, some amazing things happened.

I wish I knew more about Daddy's childhood home. For one thing, where did he learn to speak in idioms instead of normal English? Visitors in our home at mealtime looked puzzled when Daddy would say, "Would someone please pass Harley a tater?" and we would pass him the plate of biscuits. "Hold her Newt! She's headed for the barn!" meant we were to stop whatever we were doing, but "Pa! Come quick! Bell and Kate just kreed a possum up a skweetgum kree about kwenty feet high" meant we were to stop what we were doing and come see something. A whole lot of things—people, cars, houses—were "forty-eleven" of them. "Forty going north" meant someone was going very fast. If you experienced allergies in May, Dad would say, "He's a little puny in the spring." But my favorite was how he announced it when a couple decided to get married: "He let his wheel of conversation float around her axis of understanding."

Daddy spent his life working for Erwin Wholesale, selling groceries to small mom-and-pop grocery stores in Spartanburg County. Mama returned to teaching first grade, this time at Whitney Elementary School, when I was eleven. When he wasn't working, Daddy was a full-time father who gave himself to us kids. He made me a fairly good baseball player, and thanks to him I won most ping pong games I ever played. But his greatest gift to me was teaching me how to laugh at myself. I have a good laugh almost every day, just as he did.

Mama had the wonderful ability to remain calm in life's storms. She never raised her voice, ever—not to me, sister Caroline, Daddy, or any of the first graders she taught. The respect and love she gave to us was enough to keep us in line. None of us ever wanted to disappoint her or betray the love and trust she placed in us. My faith journey finally led me to embrace my mother's version of faith and her understanding of God.

Can you see why I say Caroline and I had the best parents ever? Believe me, they were a hard act to follow with our own kids.

Chapter 2

Penny

I've been hesitant to tell this story for more than fifty years, mainly because life has taught me that love relationships are always very fragile.

Marriages made in heaven can still go to hell because we are all imperfect people. Someone once said, "If you think your marriage was made in heaven, remember that lightning and thunder were made there, also." In spite of numerous difficulties, Penny and I have always been able to work our way through them, and I am so grateful we have. Maybe after fifty years of marriage I can finally share our story.

There is a common phrase my church friends use whenever something coincidental seems a bit more than that: "It was a God thing," they say. It is like saying we cannot prove it, but it looks to us like God's fingerprints are all over those circumstances. Such was the case in early September 1970.

I was a junior in college. I traveled the same road each day from my home to Wofford College. I frequently stopped at the same traffic light at the corner of North Pine Street and East Daniel Morgan Avenue, less than a mile from Wofford. I was already considering a career in ministry, and so it was quite usual that I would be engaged in conversations with God as I drove to school.

On one Monday morning, I was frustrated and angry, and I was expressing that frustration to God. Although I was having success in school and was surrounded by many friends, I didn't seem able to take the step from having "friends that were girls" to having a lasting relationship with a "girlfriend." To this twenty-year-old, that was enough to make me question God's ability to answer my prayers. So as I sat there at that light, I said out loud, "God, if you are trying to tell me that you want me to make my journey in life alone, I think we can forget it right here and now!"

There it was—I had thrown down the gauntlet. I had issued to God my "either or." I went along my way to class.

Later, on Thursday of that week as I drove to school, I again stopped at that same light. At that moment, the memory of my Monday prayer came back to me, and I began to laugh at myself. I had previously committed myself to following God's will for my life, and yet just a few days earlier I had added a conditional clause that was just plain wrong. So this time at that light I prayed, "God, please don't bring a potential girlfriend into my life until I am able to sincerely say that I will follow you, no matter what your will for me is."

I had a good laugh at myself until the light turned green.

After class that day, I popped by the home of Don and Julia, mentors in the faith and spiritual guides to countless college kids, to tell Julia about my Monday and my Thursday prayers. She joined me in having a good laugh at me and to celebrate with me the opportunity for spiritual growth I had just given myself.

Then the phone rang. It was a student returning to Converse College, and I heard Julia tell her, "Why don't you come to Bible study tonight here at our home?" Then she said, "Oh, you don't have a car. Maybe I can find you a ride ... Arthur, could you pick up Penny Nuckols tonight and bring her to Bible study?"

I said I could, but I was puzzled. I knew Penny, and she and a recent Wofford graduate were supposed to have gotten married in June.

Apparently they had called off the wedding.

So that night I went by Penny's recently married sister's apartment to chauffeur Penny to Bible study.

Penny and I had been acquaintances for two years. During my freshman year, she dated a very good friend of mine. During my sophomore year, she had been engaged to another friend of mine. We both attended a college interdenominational Christian fellowship every Sunday night, and Penny played the piano for our singing. So it wasn't all that odd that she would feel okay with me driving her to a Bible study, as we were already friends.

I invited Penny to go roller skating with my church's youth and college group the next evening, and since she knew many of those folks, she agreed to go along with me. When I showed up with an attractive Converse College senior, my friends were beside themselves in full matchmaking mode.

One of the guys said to me, "When I saw you come in with Penny, you gave me such hope. I figure if you could get someone like Penny to go out on a date with you, then maybe I had a chance, too."

Not exactly a compliment, but it was very accurate!

That's been fifty-three years ago now. We were married less than a year after our first date.

I do believe in "God things." This, I believe, was one of them.

Chapter 3

Doug Pridgeon

Other than my parents and my grandparents, I would be hard pressed to name anyone who had a greater influence on my life than Douglas Lamar Pridgeon.

For starters, we were second cousins. His grandfather Simpson Cannon and my granddaddy John Cannon were brothers who were very close. They both attended Bethel Methodist Church and raised their two large families there. The children from those two homes were as close as brothers and sisters, and consequently, the next generation was also very close. In many ways, Doug and I were like brothers. We loved one another most of the time; we fought and hated each other a few times.

A few years ago, Doug pointed to a scar on his forehead and said to his girlfriend, "Can't you tell that this scar is in the shape of Arthur's two front teeth?"

I reminded him that during another wrestling match, he had stuck his finger in my eye, which resulted in a corneal abrasion. Only one of my eyes had to have cataract surgery several years ago, and I really suspect it was caused by that injury. Many times, Doug and I walked down to Lawsons Fork Creek to see who could skip rocks the farthest; these creek adventures always degenerated into skipping rocks at each other. Somebody always got hit.

When people saw us together, they always thought Doug was several years older when, in fact, he was just two months older. Doug was always the tallest boy in his elementary school classroom, while I was always the smallest. We saw each other every week at church, and that is where our friendship grew. When we became seventh graders, we were old enough to join the Methodist Youth Fellowship and the youth choir, and this gave us three occasions each Sunday to grow our friendship. His parents were building a second home on Roan Mountain, and often I would be a guest there for the weekend. Hours spent hiking on Roan Mountain and on a section of the Appalachian Trail further cemented our friendship.

But the influence Doug had on me was because of the fact that he had very good manners and a friendly way of interacting with others. I watched him hold doors open for others, and he always seemed at ease around everyone. The Cannon clan is well known for their interpersonal skills; they were excellent teachers and salesmen, and many were excellent public speakers. Doug personified all of these Cannon traits. It was no surprise to any of his classmates that the Spartanburg High School Class of 1968 gave him the superlative of being the "Friendliest." And I tried to be just like him.

In our first year at Spartanburg High School (tenth grade), not only were we at the same school for the first time, but we also were in the same homeroom all three years. As I had done at church, I rode Doug's coattail at school. His friends became my friends, also. The next spring, Interact, one of the two service clubs for boys at our high school, invited Doug and me to join them. This was a meaningful service organization, and in part my inclusion was because of my connection to Doug (although having our cousin John already in Interact probably helped me also).

Toward the end of our junior year, Doug and I were completely caught by surprise when we were asked to co-host the weekly Scribbler Radio Show on Saturday mornings on Spartanburg's radio station WSPA-AM. *Scribbler* was the name of our monthly school newspaper, and like the paper, the radio show was a way to inform students and the community about school events. Reporters who would cover the news from clubs and sports were recruited, and it was up to Doug and me to anchor this program and make sure we had enough news and music to fill our weekly thirty-minute shows.

Only one tape of our Scribbler Radio Show survives to this day and it was one of our best—the Christmas show from late 1967. It is an absolute treasure. Doug's smooth radio voice can be heard reading a commercial (and getting tickled at himself toward the end of it), and there I am with my high voice. Other cast members and class leaders made reports that day, but the big surprise was when "Santa" arrived to read letters from well-known teachers and friends. Our friend Lee Bryant was often in school plays, so we knew he would be a great Santa. His act was great—but shorter than we expected. Doug and I realized we were out of material for that week's show and we still had about five minutes to fill. Quickly we went to a commercial break, and during that one-minute break, we decided that I would interview Santa. I jotted down a few questions, and when Lee read them, he protested that he didn't know the answers. But I knew Lee had a very quick wit and so I told him just to "fake it" and make something up. He did that very successfully, and it was one of our best and funniest segments ever.

After high school graduation and before Doug and I headed off to college, Doug got a job at our South Carolina United Methodist Camp (now known as Asbury Hills). In the summer of 1968, there was a big shortage of male counselors at camp, and since Doug was known for his leadership with Methodist Youth, he was given a job even though he was actually too young for it. Just how desperate the camp director Wes Voigt was is shown by the fact that he also offered me a job on Doug's recommendation, even though I also was too young. It was a difficult summer for me because of my small size and the fact that I looked like I was no older than the junior high campers.

It was many years later when I realized just how important that summer was for me because I met a lot of pastors who would become my colleagues a few years later when I also became a pastor. So once again, I have to give Doug credit for his influence on my life.

As I was making plans to enter the ordained ministry of The United Methodist Church, Doug was feeling another kind of call to ministry. For three years he was the Anderson, South Carolina, area director of Young Life, an organization that challenges high school students to commit their lives to Christ. A lot of lives were touched by Doug's personality, his love, and his faith.

My vocation moved me away from Spartanburg, and for most of our adult lives, our paths rarely passed. Doug's first marriage ended in divorce, and relationships between Doug and his extended Cannon family were strained during this time. I made a point of being at his marriage to his second wife, Jane, because I knew I would be his only family present.

I was also there with him the day after Jane died in her sleep in 2017. Remembering our close friendship, a high school classmate called to tell me the news and to suggest I drive across the county to be there with Doug that day. Of course, I wanted to be there.

During those days, I was able to reconnect with his two grown children, Brian and Lauren. I marveled at the way Brian earned his annual income during the few months of summer by working for a large commercial fishing company in Alaska, and I enjoyed being with Lauren and getting to know her baby daughter who loved her granddaddy dearly.

The next spring, our high school fiftieth class reunion gave us a good chance to reconnect again, and that was a good time for both of us as we enjoyed hearing what our childhood friends had been up to since we graduated in 1968. I watched Doug do what he always did best—move from person to person around the room to meet and greet all our classmates. He still deserved the "Friendliest" superlative.

At the reunion, I think he was also shopping for a new girlfriend! He didn't find one there, but he did find Linda near his job at an insurance company in Lyman. One day he called to ask Penny and me to join them for dinner one evening. They seemed to have gotten serious very fast, and there was an interesting story to explain that. Linda had invited Doug to supper to get to know her family, and Doug was having trouble keeping his diabetes in check. As he waited for the meal to be served, he passed out! EMS came rushing to the house, and they stripped him of most of his clothes so they could get wires, monitors, and IV fluids going. Doug said he woke up lying in a bed, mostly naked, and surrounded by medics and Linda's family!

"After that," Doug said, "we all felt like we knew each other pretty well."

I will finish my tribute to my dear friend Doug with a story about our playing on a church league softball team just before we went to college. Doug, being a lefty, played first base, of course. I played second base because I had years of Little League experience playing that position. Often when a fly ball is hit between two players, one of them will call it for themselves. Rarely a player will ask another player to catch it instead of him. On this occasion, the fly ball was hit down the first base line just a few feet fair—obviously a ball for the first baseman to catch. But for some reason, Doug began yelling my name. I ran over to back him up, but he was in front of me and the ball was coming down in front of him. He continued to call my name in spite of the fact that I would have to knock him out of the way to be able to catch the pop up. The ball hit the ground and landed in his glove on one hop, and then Doug turned around quickly and said to me, "Arthur, why didn't you catch that ball?" I just gave him a puzzled look, and he realized he should have caught it. We repeated that story year after year, each one of us blaming the other for the error!

The last time I kidded Doug about this was when we were seventy-one years old and Doug was in a nursing home facing his final days. On October 30, 2021, this very influential friend for all my life died. A few days later, I officiated at a graveside service for Doug, which was attended by many of our cousins, his daughter, and our high school classmates. Doug was quite a guy.

Chapter 4

Mike Blanton

In fall 1956, I almost became a school dropout while in the first grade thanks to Mike Blanton.

We sat at tables that year, four kids per table. Two girls, Mike, and I shared one table, and Mike loved to make the girls squeal and laugh by turning his eyelids inside out. Their squeals always brought our teacher, Miss Hammett, rushing over to our table, where she would stand Mike up from his chair and give him one spank with her hand. It never seemed to faze him, but it scared me to death. Each time Miss Hammett marched over to our table, I just knew she was coming to get me because I had laughed at Mike, too.

After she spanked Mike and sat him back down in his chair, I would raise my hand and say that I had to go to the boys' bathroom. But I would walk past the restroom down to my sister's fourth grade classroom and ask her to go to the office and call Mama to come get me because I was done for the day!

The next time Mike was spanked and I raised my hand, Miss Hammett sent another boy along with me to make sure that I went only to the restroom, but he wasn't big enough to stop me when I ran down the hall to Caroline's classroom again. Mom had to resort to bribes to get me to stay in school; there would be a cheap toy waiting on me if I didn't try to run away.

Mike came from a very fine, very devout family of Wesleyans. My family was quite devout also, but Wesleyans were stricter than Methodists in those days. Wesleyans didn't go to movies, and many didn't have a television. In junior high school, when the boys' and girls' gym classes were allowed (or made) to dance, members of certain churches were allowed to run laps around the football field instead. As a result of all that running, Mike became an excellent athlete, excelling in tumbling and basketball. He was a member of the Spartanburg High School varsity basketball team that won the state championship in 1968. And Mike became well known as a quiet but popular young man.

But what I most remember about him is that if something bad was going to happen to anyone on the playground during recess, it was going to happen to Mike. He was "that guy." Usually it was not his fault at all; he was just at the wrong place at the wrong time. And whatever it was that happened, it always ended up breaking Mike's glasses.

Take, for instance, the time we were breaking the school rules by playing ball at recess with a real baseball instead of the mandated softball. The two fourth grade classes and the two fifth grade classes had recess at the same time and same place, and there were several different ball games going on at the same time on that small field. While our group was playing with that baseball, Mike was walking on the other side of that playground on a driveway, which was usually beyond the reach of everything except ground balls that occasionally rolled that far. He was just walking one way and running back the other way, minding his own business. Just then, the batter hit a towering fly ball to deep center field! That baseball traveled much higher and farther than a softball would have, and we all stopped playing to watch Mike and the falling baseball on collision course. We were frozen in disbelief, but we could see what was about to happen. Sure enough, that baseball hit Mike right on the top of his head. His glasses flew off his face and broke, and Mike was almost knocked out cold (and our baseball was confiscated by the principal, of course).

The next year Mike was sitting on the on-deck rock, waiting for his turn at bat during recess in the sixth grade. The current batter tried to check his swing, and he fouled the softball directly at Mike. It hit him right between the eyes, breaking his glasses at the nose bridge! Vannerson Opticians in the Montgomery Building kept glasses and frames in readiness for Mike at all times.

We went our separate ways after high school. My career was in the church, and Mike joined his father as an insurance salesman. We both had sons at Boiling Springs High School when we renewed our friendship, and our boys both played on the varsity soccer team. For a school assignment, his son Jody was interviewing people in various careers, and I was honored that he interviewed me to learn more about the work of a pastor. I could tell Jody was a young man who was deeply committed to his faith, and I knew where that had come from.

A decade later, I retired and returned to Boiling Springs. I had learned the place to go to meet an interesting variety of people was Waffle House, and that's where I ran into Mike again. By now, he had put on a few pounds, as we say, and also grown a very long beard. Most of the time, Mike was with the same small group, eating breakfast and studying the Bible. Occasionally he would come by himself and sit at the high counter with me.

There was just one topic that Mike was interested in pursuing, and that was what he and I were doing to grow spiritually and to help others grow. At that time, he was hosting small groups in his home, attempting to make more deeply dedicated disciples than he was finding in area churches, but he was also interested in the interim pastoral work I was doing in retirement. Mike was always very serious and single-minded about his faith, and I am sure he wondered about me, a pastor who loves to laugh and tell jokes. But the truth is that both of us hoped to make disciples, each in our own way.

In one of our conversations, I learned his soccer-playing son was married and living in Indonesia as a teacher. In that Muslim country, people have to be very careful about sharing their faith, but that was why Jody was there. Again, I knew where that young man had gotten his passion for sharing the Good News.

In the decade since I retired, Mike and his wife have both died. Deborah, a retired schoolteacher with many friends in our community, died in 2018, and her funeral service was conducted by her sons. That fact says a lot! Mike died four years later. In his obituary, his church membership was listed as "the body of Christ." I think that was his way of saying he saw himself as one who was connected with every Christian in every church and not someone who was limited by any church's doctrines.

Perhaps if I had learned how to turn my eyelids inside-out, I could have been as fine a man as Mike.

Chapter 5

Whitney's Steve Cannon

Another childhood friend who had a major influence on me was my classmate for sixteen years, Steve Cannon from Whitney, South Carolina. From first grade in 1956 until our graduation from Wofford College in 1972, we were friends. Steve influenced not only me but also every other boy in our elementary school.

In first and second grade, we ran around during recess and played tag, or else we were on the old jungle gym. But by the third grade, thanks to Steve, we all wanted to play baseball every chance we had. My father had begun my baseball training, but it was Steve's contagious love for baseball that made it my favorite sport. He was way ahead of all of us. If you went to visit him on a Saturday, whatever you were doing had to stop so he could watch the baseball game of the week. Steve prepared a score sheet to record each player's stats, just like the one printed in the newspaper. Keeping score was serious business with Steve. Baseball was serious with him, too.

Steve had a baseball glove with a well-formed pocket that we all wanted our gloves to look just like, and he showed us exactly how to achieve this. We had to use special leather oil, place a ball in the pocket, and wrap a belt around it overnight to get the glove broken in just right. If your glove had a player's signature on it (mine was

Don Blasingame), Steve knew the team he played for (St. Louis Cardinals). The fact that Blasingame played second base sealed my fate. That became my primary position by the time I was ten and playing Little League ball.

Coach Jerry Mahar, the physical education coach at Whitney School, was one of my all-time favorite teachers. One of the things he did that was above and beyond the call of duty was to hold softball tournaments every spring between the two fifth and the two sixth grade classes. Without any challengers for that job, Steve took charge of our fifth-grade team, assigning us our positions and arranging the batting order. He was our shortstop, and I was the second baseman. Our team was absolutely awesome! We lost a few games but won the championship that first year. The second year, we went undefeated on our way to another championship.

Steve and I played on different teams in the Little League. I was drafted by a neighbor whose son played for the team sponsored by the Civitan civic club, while Steve was a star for the ABC team. Since he played second base for his team, I would have sat on the bench a lot if I had not joined a rival team. Occasionally he pitched, and one time I hit an inside-the-park home run off him—the highlight of my Little League career.

My mother sure was happy that Steve also was responsible for me wanting to get to school very early every day. I wanted to be there in time to join the other boys in playing a game called "Little Tip." In this version of baseball, the pitcher would toss the spongy ball to the batter, and if the batter hit the ball at all—even a foul tip—he had to run to first base and back to home plate without being thrown out. Although you could be tagged out by a fielder, the usual manner of being called "out" was to be hit by the ball as you ran the baseline. In that way it was a combination of baseball and dodge ball. This formed the basis of games of kickball and Little Tip that we played many afternoons in my backyard after school.

Steve continued to advance in his skills, eventually playing for our high school and Wofford College's baseball teams. I was very small for my age, and once I went up against thirteen- to fifteen-year-olds in the next level, I couldn't compete. I resorted to many years of church league softball, even some fast-pitch softball, finally quitting when I hit forty (years, not home runs).

There would be other great mentors who would leave their mark on me, but Steve gave many of us a love for the healthy sport of baseball. He was an excellent student, too, and we all tried to be just like him on both counts.

If anything about Steve surprised me, it was that he didn't get the chance to play professional baseball. He was the best ballplayer I ever saw.

Chapter 6

The Backyard Gang

Our backyard at my childhood home was very large, with a series of rolling hills and flat places where my sister Caroline and I, plus all our Baby Boomer neighbors, gathered to play. We had a swing set on an upper plateau. Both the front and back yards were made of packed red clay soil. Poor Dad never did get grass to grow in either yard because of the stomping of little feet.

Although there were several level areas to play on, our favorite place was on the flat area closest to the house (and to Mama's Kool-Aid).

If the game had a ball, we played it. We were especially fond of kickball, baseball, and dodgeball. The common element in all those games was the back of our house that kept our ball from rolling way down the hill to the street. Our house was sided with shingles—green asbestos shingles—and many of those shingles became casualties of our games. Most of the time we would run to only one base and then back to the home plate (a large square cement block).

First base was the gutter on the corner of the house, which didn't work too well as a gutter after it got stomped flat. The runner was out if the ball was thrown at and hit him or her, and that was the best part of these games. But many times, the throw missed its mark and hit the side of the house instead and broke another shingle.

I have often thought about those backyard games and the many lessons we learned by playing together. Ricky was my best friend from the time I was four and he was three. Lee was two years younger, a rough and tough kid who could break any toy and wear out a bicycle tire in short order. Bobby and his next-door neighbor Gary were bigger than the rest of us, and they really disliked each other—a lot. They often acted out their dislike of each other in our games, especially dodgeball. Either of them could throw the ball hard enough to take your feet out from under you, but they delighted in blistering each other's legs with that stinging dodge ball. And when they missed their target, the ball hit a shingle of the house and ... well, you know.

Then there was Rhonda, my girlfriend. While riding our bikes one day when we were nine, she told me she liked me and asked if I liked her. I was at that "girls have cooties" age, so I was okay with our shared fondness for each other just as long as she kept a respectable distance from me. But she was a good ballplayer, so she was always on my team. Her little brother Robby and his friend Eric also joined in those games. There was a wide age-span in that group.

Since a pastor has to get along with a variety of people—and help them get along—my backyard was the place I first learned how to help people get along. It wasn't always easy. Usually I could break up an argument by doing something funny. My mother had been a director of Christian education, and she saw our backyard as an extension of her former career, so she was able to help me learn. We practiced our own voluntary form of "affirmative action" because we knew it wasn't fair to pitch the baseball as fast to the little kids as we did to older, more experienced batters. Clearly the object of our play was for everybody to have fun; it really didn't matter who was the best or who won. What mattered was our friendship.

Some of the things we learned in my backyard were the rules of baseball and sports terminology. One time a younger kid was on base, and he continued to stand there after his teammate had gotten a hit.

"Run home, Eric!" I hollered.

He did!

He ran past home plate, down the driveway, up the street, and into his house.

A few minutes later, he came back, red-faced and mad, wanting to fight me.

"My mother wasn't calling me," he complained. "Why did you tell me to run home?"

But he joined us in a good laugh when he learned that "home" was the name of a base.

Our baseball games took on greater importance in 1961 when Mickey Mantle and Roger Maris were in a slugfest to see which of them would break Babe Ruth's home run record. My favorite team, the Yankees, was headed for the World Series, too, and we were all so excited. My Little League number was nine, the same as Maris's, and I was beyond thrilled when he hit home run number sixty-one.

Lee had an older brother who would try to get him to go home as the sun set by telling him, "You'd better come on home right now or else the ghosts and goblins will get you!" Most of the time, I was ready for Lee to go home before he broke something else of mine, and so I didn't contradict his older brother. But I felt sorry for him one evening as night was falling, and I decided that "the truth shall set you free."

I said to Lee, "Tell your brother there are no such things as ghosts or goblins!"

He did, and we kept playing. But after it got totally dark, I went inside the house and left him outside, all alone.

No ghosts were going to get me!

Chapter 7

Mrs. Thompson and Her Mistletoe

My fourth-grade teacher, Mrs. Ethel Thompson, was one of my all-time favorite teachers because she enjoyed laughter and fun. Every Christmas season, she would hang mistletoe over the door to her classroom, and if we walked into the classroom as close to the sides of the door as possible, we were safe. But if we forgot and walked right under the middle of the door (and the mistletoe), Mrs. Thompson would plant a big old kiss right on us! Since we boys that age didn't want much to do with being kissed by our teacher, we were her primary targets.

Mrs. Thompson's favorite thing to do was see some boy she knew from another classroom—perhaps a boy she had taught in a previous year—and call his name as he walked down the hall, telling him to come into her classroom. Of course, the boy would obey, and no sooner would he get under the mistletoe than Mrs. Thompson would smooch him. Very often the boy would flee the scene as fast as he could while we all laughed loudly! Mrs. Thompson loved it.

One time it backfired on her, and then it backfired on us. Our school custodian, Howard (the only person of color I knew at our school), walked into our classroom and stood motionless right under the mistletoe. We all pointed at him and laughed loudly, and Mrs. Thompson turned red in the face. As soon as Howard left, Mrs.

Thompson gave us a scolding we wouldn't soon forget—plus extra homework to boot!

Back in the late 1980s when I was approaching my fortieth birthday, I was invited to speak at Bethel United Methodist Church in Spartanburg at a midweek Lenten service. Looking out at the people in attendance, I saw Mrs. Thompson sitting there with two other former teachers of mine, including one from Cleveland Junior High School, Mrs. Emily Martin, who had helped me reconcile faith and science. (As she explained, "Faith tries to answer the question who created the universe and why; science tries to discover how it came into existence.") Somehow I managed to deliver my message without too many goofs or too much nervousness.

After the service, Mrs. Thompson shook my hand and said, "Well, that was a little bit better than all those book reports you used to read to the class!"

During that sermon, I had also told a story about my third grade teacher, Evelyn Bell, and how I watched her change a boy's life through a gift of grace after he had stolen someone's baseball glove (again). The principal whipped him, of course, but Mrs. Bell had us all contribute yellow "Top Value Stamps" so the class could get the young boy his own baseball glove. Her act of grace succeeded where threats of punishment had failed. That day, following my sermon, her fellow schoolteachers called Mrs. Bell and told her about the story about her that I had told.

Later that day, I received a short phone call from Mrs. Bell. As I remember it, she said, "This is Mrs. Bell. You are doing my funeral! Bye." About twenty years later, I did. And of course, I told that story at her funeral and later included it in my second book, *People of My Journey*.

I had some wonderful schoolteachers.

Chapter 8

Jimmy Bozard

My best college buddy was a boy from St. Matthews, South Carolina—or "Say-int Mah-thoose," as he said in his Lowcountry drawl. He also pronounced my name as "Oi-tha," and that took some adjustments in my listening skills. I moved into Greene Hall midway through my sophomore year at Wofford into the room next to Jimmy Bozard and Freddie "Frog" Stabler, his friend from his hometown.

On the day I moved in, my two neighbors and some of their friends decided to welcome me with a series of practical jokes. One of the jokes was giving me a "pink belly" by holding me down and pouring a cola on my bare stomach and then slapping my belly until it was stinging and very red! They were laughing loudly and I was yelling loudly, and that was enough to disturb another neighbor down the hall—a football player who was a very serious pre-med student. He yelled from his room loud enough to be heard through his closed door and over all of our yelling, "HOLT! HOLT!"

You should have seen the way those other guys ran back to their rooms and slammed their doors as if they were very afraid of the wrath that was about to come upon them from that huge football player.

Jimmy and I became close friends in a very short time. He recruited me to be the second baseman on an intramural softball team (he was the first baseman). We double-dated (and once triple-dated). He was the life of the party always.

Jim always thought he did worse on exams than he actually did; he really was a very good student. When I would ask him how the exam was, he would always pat himself on his backside as he said, "If you see it floating around campus, tie it to a tree until I can come get it." But what he was perhaps best known for was the wads of wet paper towels or wet toilet paper he could toss from the corner shower room and hit moving targets walking across campus. A professor with an umbrella was asking for it! I learned not to open my dorm window—it cranked open to the side—because more than once a paper I was writing got ruined by a wet ball. A successful attack always resulted in a high-pitched laugh that could be heard across campus.

The summer after we had been dorm neighbors, Jimmy invited me to visit him at his parents' home in St. Matthews, and he introduced me to his favorite Saturday night activity—cruising. He would drive his car between two locations in Orangeburg, looking for girls. If he found someone he wanted to meet, he would drive into the Piggie Park and wait to see if the other car followed. Since I had just spilled a milkshake all over myself, I decided that it was best if we did not approach the occupants of the car next to his that evening!

Penny and I were married just before my senior year at Wofford. The nonfraternity "Independent" group that sponsored our softball team also sponsored a nominee for homecoming queen every year, and that year (1971) I was so proud that they asked my lovely new bride to be their nominee. This probably was a first—a married nominee for homecoming queen—and this was all Jimmy's doing.

After graduation, we both ended up in Columbia, South Carolina, a few years later. I was in seminary, and he was working for the state mental health department. We would often meet for lunches to catch up on old times. When Penny and I had our first baby, Jimmy mailed a cute dress for our baby girl along with two notes. My note said, "I know you are very proud of your daughter!" Penny's note said, "I am surprised at you! I told you to keep away from Arthur!"

The year following the baby's birth, I received a phone call from a fellow pastor who was a friend of Jimmy's older brother, informing me Jimmy had suffered a massive aneurysm at the base of his brain and was on life support. I joined the vigil at the hospital. I spent hours in prayer. Apparently Jimmy had become "brain dead" within minutes of that ruptured aneurysm, and soon we gathered for his funeral.

Jimmy wasn't the first close friend I had lost, but his death hit me especially hard. My faith seriously quaked in the year following his death. All my seminary training didn't seem to offer me any answers. I wanted to leave the ministry. But I have always been fortunate to be surrounded by many wise mentors, and they helped me grow in my faith and understanding.

In my book, *What I Have Come to Believe*, I wrote these words that reflect my new faith perspective resulting from Jim's death:

> If God is all-knowing, all-present, and all-powerful, then how could anything outside of God's control ever happen? My answer is that God has put some self-imposed limits upon God's power. Why would the Almighty do that? It would be necessary if God's desire was for us—and all creatures—to experience freedom, autonomy, love, and meaning. Puppets on strings experience perfect orderliness, always under the control of the puppeteer. But they could never experience meaning, and God wanted us to be fully alive. To be able to experience love and meaning, we must also know what it feels like to experience the lack of love and the absence of meaning. Life isn't fully appreciated until one realizes that death is a possibility. It appears to me that God has decreed some self-imposed limits so that we might have free will.

Perhaps the greatest influence Jimmy had on my life was not all the laughter, not the dodging of wet paper wads, not the softball games, but the renewed faith that his death caused me to experience.

I really owe him.

Part 2
Mentors

Chapter 9

Addendum to the Story about Doug Bowling

In the first book, Theophilus,"—that is, in my book *People of My Journey*—I wrote about my friend and mentor Doug Bowling. But I decided to leave out one of the best parts of that story because it contained something that could have been seen as criticism of one of our United Methodist churches.

However, that church has since disaffiliated and is no longer a United Methodist church, which frees me from that earlier concern. Here is the rest of the story for you now.

In 2001, Buncombe Street UMC was to receive a change in pastoral leadership. Integral to this story is the nature of that church.

At the time, Buncombe Street UMC was at the very top of our ecclesiastical food chain. The pastor's salary and the church's reputation made it the common goal of all pastors who aspire to climbing up the church spire, so to speak.

As such, the church was accustomed to telling the bishop who they wanted as their pastor, and they were accustomed to getting who they asked for.

This time, the church's Staff-Parish Relations Committee told District Superintendent Gareth Scott that they wanted—and expected—that Dr. Will Willimon would be appointed as their new pastor.

At that time, Dr. Willimon was the dean of the chapel at Duke University and a professor there, and he was also being considered for the office of bishop.

Scott talked with Bishop Lawrence McCleskey, who wisely suggested that Gareth contact Willimon to see if he was interested in leaving his highly visible and important position at Duke to become the pastor of Buncombe Street, and he was not—at all—interested. So the next time Gareth met with the SPRC and again they said that Willimon was to be their next pastor, Gareth had to tell them Willimon had turned them down.

As a result, Doug was appointed as their pastor.

The first time Doug met with the SPRC, someone said to him, "How does it feel to be our second choice?"

Doug quickly replied, "It feels sort of like it must have felt for you to be turned down by Willimon."

Chapter 10

Wes Voigt

I finally grew up in the summer of 1968 as a young counselor at the South Carolina United Methodist Camp (before it was known as "Asbury Hills"). I was eighteen and looked every bit of twelve, maybe thirteen. I was short (I grew six inches during college) and immature (I still am). My voice had not yet changed, but I lost my high-pitched voice that summer thanks to yelling to be heard by the youth. I started Wofford a few months later almost sounding like a male of the species. I am sure the only reason Wes Voigt hired me was that he was desperate. He had very few male counselors that summer. In fact, if it had not been for the male pastors who gave the camp a week of their time away from their parishes, we would have been extremely shorthanded.

I was struggling to piece together my basic beliefs at that time, and in retrospect that summer at camp was absolutely vital to my future career as a United Methodist pastor. It was there that I met some people I would spend my life with in our collegial family—George Fields, Richard McAlister, Archie Bigelow, John and Wally Culp, James Ellis Griffeth, Eugene Eaddy, Bob Strother, Al Spradley, Bob Tanner, Joe Alley, musician Betty Bradham Doll, and many others. One evening as I was moving my washed clothes over to the dryer, I observed Mike Alexander—our sixteen-year-old camp dishwasher—

talking with one of our lovely camp counselors, Betsy Sparrow. He must have been a persuasive talker because they got married a few years later!

One thing these pastors uniformly demonstrated to me that summer was that loving people of other races was not something that was being tacked onto the Christian faith in the 1960s. Rather, it was so vital that without it you don't have Christian faith at all. Loving God and loving our neighbor as ourselves is Christianity.

That summer we built a few of the many trails that are still used at Asbury Hills. Occasionally we would hear a single pistol shot, and we would know that Wes had just killed another copperhead. We found a large den of them as we were clearing the land right next to the dining hall.

After I became an ordained pastor, Wes would see me every year at Annual Conference, making a point of inviting me to return to camp to be a counselor for a week. He either had a poor memory or a heart of grace. I was a very poor counselor.

Wes deserves all the accolades he has been given in establishing our camp. Dolly hasn't gotten nearly as many as she deserves as the manager of the kitchen and preparer of all of the meals. Their children made their own important contributions to our camp. We owe them all our thanks.

These thoughts came to me after I read of Wes's death in the *South Carolina United Methodist Advocate* in July 2022. I wonder how many others besides me found direction for their lives and grew up just a bit under the guidance of Wes Voigt?

Chapter 11

Carl Clary and the College Place Youth

In the spring of my freshman year at Wofford, I was invited to participate in a Lay Witness Mission at College Place United Methodist Church in Columbia, South Carolina. They invited us college students because they wanted us to lead the discussion groups for the youth of the church. Since I was thinking about becoming a youth minister, this seemed a good step for my own growth.

Lay Witness Missions are about lay members of various churches spending the weekend as guests of the host church. We stayed in the homes of the host church's members, and in those homes and in gatherings at church, we shared stories of our faith journey with each other. The hope was that someone who was struggling with some aspect of their faith would find someone they could identify with and grow as a result of that friendship.

On Saturday nights of these events, there was a time when people were invited to spend some time in prayer in the sanctuary before returning to their homes. For some people, this was a time for rededication and renewal.

On this particular night, I noticed a group of high school girls kneeling together. Before long, they began embracing one another. There was laughter and some tears. It seemed like there was something very special and very real happening to these youth.

But what I hadn't seen very often was what those young ladies did next. They left the kneeling rail and went out in the halls and into the church yard to find their friends and invite them to come join them in prayer. On one of their trips outside to recruit more youth, the girls swarmed around Pat, a high school boy who seemed to be a bit of a loner. What high school boy could have refused such an attractive invitation to pray? But something very real was happening to Pat, also. Soon I saw him talking to one of the college students about beginning a new life of dedicated discipleship.

On Sunday after the worship service, we all headed home. But a few weeks after this weekend event, one of my college friends told me that the pastor, the Reverend Carl Clary, wanted one of us to come spend the summer working with the youth of the church. I was the only one who had no summer plans, and so I was happy to accept his invitation. I would be staying in a guest bedroom in the parsonage with Carl and his wife, Ann, and their two sons, Bobby and Doug. Since College Place Church is on the campus of Columbia College (a school for girls only at that time), I got to eat all my meals in the college dining hall with the young ladies every day. I know what you are thinking—it was a tough job but somebody had to do it.

I had absolutely no training for this job at all other than growing up in a church with a very active youth group, so I tried to create a youth group like my own back home. I copied the Bible studies and fellowship activities like the ones I had grown up doing. There were adult workers who led youth events, and my primary job was to help them. There were two groups of teenagers in the church—an older group of eleventh and twelfth graders and a younger group of middle schoolers. All I knew to do was to offer myself as a friend to these youth, and that seemed to be enough.

This was the "Summer of '69" (to borrow a song title from Bryan Adams). The older group had lost several high school friends in Vietnam who had been drafted right after graduation. Those deaths hit the youth very hard. Several times, our Sunday night youth meetings became times for us to deal with their grief. But there were other times that were much happier—like Sunday, July 20, 1969. I was with that older youth group in one of their homes while together we watched television as Neil Armstrong took his "one giant leap for mankind." I waited for just the right moment to sing the CCR song, "I see a bad [earth] rising."

But it was with the younger group that I spent most of my time. Pat was one of the anchors of this group; he seemed to have many friends now. Pat lived in the College Place neighborhood and came to see me almost every day. He would ride with me in my English Ford Cortina as we visited the church's inactive youth and invited them to come to our youth meetings. We would eat burgers together and talk about life, the Bible, and growing in faith.

A group of boys from another United Methodist church on the opposite side of Columbia traveled over to this younger youth group, and I knew that I was not the source of the attraction. The budding romances were fun to watch. Paul and Jep were two of these across-town travelers, and they added so much to this group. But most of the members of this younger group lived in the church neighborhood.

One afternoon each week we would meet at the church for our "Sharing Group." I had a cheap guitar back them, and I was still trying to learn to make it my partner in youth ministry. I would lead a few minutes of singing and then present some passage from the Bible for study, and then the youth were free to share problems and exciting stories about their spiritual journey. We would end with prayer. We also met on Sunday evenings.

After six weeks, it was time for summer to end and school to resume. I experienced what would someday become a repeated heartbreak as I left behind a church that I loved to move to another church. It never got easier. I always left a part of my heart at the church I was leaving.

I still hear from a few of these youth via email and social media. Pat became an ordained pastor in another denomination and then later surprised me by his growing interest in pursuing higher education, eventually becoming quite the Koine Greek scholar. He ended up teaching courses in a college in the West. Jep, Gregg, and Paul are Facebook friends.

They still mean so much to me because I learned so much from them.

Chapter 12

The Reverend John Rowland

When I decided to give church work another try (after driving a bread truck in Virginia), I knew I needed a good mentor and a good church. At Union United Methodist Church in Irmo, I found both. Actually, I found a host of mentors and a wonderful church.

I have always kidded the senior pastor, the Reverend Julian Lazar, because he kept disappearing on me. He hired me in March 1972 at Lyman United Methodist and moved to another church three months later. Then he hired me in Irmo, and on my first day on the job—May 19, 1975—his wife's brother suffered a serious injury and was near death in a hospital in Winchester, Kentucky, and they had to rush there to see about him. After two weeks, his condition improved enough for Julian and Sara to return home with just enough time to pack themselves and their two sons for a pulpit exchange in England. So again, Julian disappeared! But we were fortunate to receive in the pulpit exchange the Reverend John Rowland, his wife Joan, and their teenage children Noel and Phillipa. John became a very wise mentor who I have always appreciated, even though he lives "across the pond."

I had only been on the job for less than a month and didn't know what I was supposed to do yet, but I was sure I was expected to help get the Rowlands settled into our parsonage and community. Penny and I went to the Greyhound Bus station to pick them and their luggage up.

Greyhound Bus, you say? You read that correctly! I am not sure what caused the Rowlands to travel by Greyhound in the summer heat and bumpy roads. They might have heard how stretched the church's finances were and wanted to save the church some expenses associated with this pastoral exchange. But whatever the reason, flying into New York and then riding a bus to South Carolina showed on their tired faces. Penny and I took them to the parsonage in Irmo where they were greeted by members of the church. I am sure they would have preferred postponing those introductions until after showers, naps, and a meal!

There was a meeting of pastors coming up early the next week, and I was asked to take John to that meeting and introduce him to our district superintendent and to the pastors of the district. After that meeting, I took John to the Baptist Hospital so he could receive a picture ID that would allow him to visit our hospitalized church members.

We entered the hospital through a side door and walked up one flight of stairs. Then John froze in front of a sign that really puzzled him: "No Soliciting."

He asked me, "What does that mean?"

I explained the hospital did not allow salespeople to bother patients, but I wondered why he had asked. It seems one of the many words that have different meanings in England and America was the word "soliciting."

John replied, "Well, I had heard that it was a prominent problem here in your country, but I didn't think it was such a big problem that it had to be outlawed in your hospitals!"

My dad had prepared me to watch out for words we Americans and folks from England both use that have very different meanings—words like "lorries," "lifts," and "the boot of a car," but I never was quite sure when I was going to make a vocal transgression of British verbiage. The last thing I wanted to do was accidentally offend our special guests!

The Rowlands were an immediate hit with the congregation and staff of Union Church. Members entertained them, sending them to the beach for a few days and to the mountains for other days. Since I worked with the youth, I made sure Phillipa and Noel were included in all youth activities. Joan entertained some of us privately with her musical skills on our church organ—I can't remember if she actually played it at a worship service. But I remember she could beautifully play sacred music and also a bit of honky-tonk if the occasion arose. And as I followed John around as he ministered to our flock, I learned so much.

I witnessed how skillfully John handled serious problems in a church in July of his six-week stay. A conflict developed between our educational director and a children's Sunday school teacher over the teacher's use of unofficial curriculum materials. Our staff member had tried to encourage the use of better, more age-appropriate lessons, but the teacher persisted in her use of unapproved and often offensive lesson materials. Finally, nothing would do other than to replace that teacher with another, and that teacher did not accept what she called "being fired" very well. Her attacks on our educational director were fierce. Being a staff member of very little experience, I was looking for a win-win solution, but John deflated that hope immediately.

"These situations almost always end with someone leaving the church," he warned us.

He encouraged us to manage the conflict by being caring toward the teacher and supportive of the staff member until Julian got back.

John's preaching was a big hit, too. His beautiful English accent caused us all to listen more carefully to his sermons. I saw a stream of young adults coming by to speak with him. I got the feeling some of them—especially the young women—were looking for a father figure who could help them heal some childhood scars. The district superintendent noticed how popular John's preaching was and tried to talk him into moving to South Carolina and becoming a United Methodist pastor here. I think John was tempted. Salaries are much better here than in England. But after six weeks, the Rowlands returned to the UK. They would make several return trips during the next few years. Each time they returned, John would be invited to speak at Union UMC, and Penny and I made sure to be there.

For almost fifty years, John has continued to mentor me by letters and emails. He sent me a book that had made a huge impact on him, *The Word and the Words*, by Colin Morris. Back in the 1970s, it was often said that local church pastors were going to be replaced by a few great preachers whose sermons would be broadcast into churches on huge movie screens. To a small degree, this has actually happened. Preachers in churches far away are being streamed via Internet to satellite churches all over the place. But the main thing that kept this from really catching on was the ability of local pastors to do something TV preachers could not do—actually get to know (and become known by) their church members on a personal level. Illustrations for sermons arising from events in local communities are always more illuminating than stories about events from far across America.

John wanted to make sure I was going to take preaching more seriously than many of my peers. It was important, as Colin Morris wrote, for the word of God to be expressed in the words of the people or else they won't understand it. John made this point every time he preached. The value he placed on preaching energized my own passion for preaching as I began my first year in seminary a month after he returned to England.

I have often used this Morris quote from *The Word and the Words*:

> Trinity Sunday is the preacher's Waterloo. If he is prudent, he will go down with a strategic bout of influenza the preceding day. If he suffers from a stern sense of duty, he will be forced to tie himself in verbal knots grappling with the ultimate mystery of God's nature. Indeed, the church could make an

honest penny charging militant atheists an admission fee for the pleasure of seeing and hearing Christian preachers battle their way through an intellectual maze, which, at whatever point they enter it, soon has them helplessly lost. This is one Sunday of the Christian year when the organist cannot afford to doze gently through the sermon, for he never knows when he will have to answer the preacher's distress signal by playing the opening bars of the final hymn—preferably double forte—to drown out the sound of groans of exhaustion from the pulpit.

Thank you, Rev. John Rowland, for your almost fifty years of friendship and guidance.

Chapter 13

The Reverend Joe Alley

I was still a teenager when I first met Joe Alley, who was at that time a recent graduate of Asbury Theological Seminary and a newly minted United Methodist pastor. I was a counselor at our Methodist camp in the summer of 1968 when we first met; I met so many of my future colleagues at camp that summer.

It was Joe's appearance that caught my attention. His hair was short, and his face looked somewhat like a sculptor had fashioned it. His countenance was serious, and he appeared to be deep in thought. I remember thinking something about him reminded me of a Native American. But his most noticeable feature was his very deep-set eyes.

A little boy once asked Joe, "Doe, why are doe eyes doe far back in doe head?"

In a few years, Joe softened his appearance by adding a gray beard.

I attended several workshops that Joe led during my early days in ministry. After completing seminary, I was invited to join a group of ten young pastors to study "Organizational Development," a workshop Joe was leading. OD is a study of how people relate to other people and to organizations, as well as how organizations relate to each other. It also offers a new model to the standard hierarchical top-down model often found in American businesses and organizations. OD's approach is much more collegial, encouraging people to relate as peers or equals. It also teaches clarity in our choice of words so we accurately express in words what we are trying to say.

For example, if we said, "You can do that," Joe would correct us to say, "One can do that" so that we would accurately be saying "anyone" rather than a "you" who was there in our group. If someone asked, "May I be excused?" Joe would say "Adults don't need other adults to give them permission to be excused."

In addition to teaching us about communication skills, Joe led us in learning about personality types and growing in self-understanding and awareness. It was in this class that I first learned about the "Johari Window" (which we learned was named for two guys, Joe and Harry, who created this model). The Johari Window has four window panes in it to help a person grow in self-awareness. One pane represents things that everybody—the person and others—is aware of. The second pane is a "blind spot," things that the person is unaware of but is known by others. The third pane is a hidden or private area known to the person but not to others. The final pane is the unknown "blind" area that neither the person nor others know about him or her. Those who want to grow in self-awareness are challenged to learn from others and share hidden things with others, as well as to take personality tests to learn more about themselves.

Communication theory was a fascinating area of study also. Based on how radio transmissions work, we learned that there are so many places where the "radio signal" can be lost or distorted as it travels from one person to another. An idea in my brain has to be encoded with words and phrases, and I may not choose the best words to express that idea. Then I may have an accent or speech impediment that creates "static" in my transmission, or perhaps I speak too softly or loudly or my false teeth slip! When my words get to your ears, you may not hear well enough to process my words. Perhaps a child cries or a horn blows, and this "static" interferes with your "receiver." Your brain tries to translate the words that you heard into ideas in your brain, and your brain may not end up receiving the idea I intended at all.

One of my friends said he was surprised to find his new girlfriend was not at all shy like he had expected her to be. All of her friends had said she was shy, but my friend used the word "backwards" to mean shyness. His new girlfriend understood "backwards" to mean "dumb," and so she burst out crying at the idea that her friends had this low opinion of her. After a few minutes of dialogue, all was well.

Joe taught us that we need to learn to ask questions about what we have heard so we can get clarity instead of getting angry. This feedback is a necessary part of communication that we are never taught.

Joe also taught us that "every brain thinks that every other brain thinks exactly as it does." By learning about personality types, we learned that no two people experience the world in the same way. We learned to use the understanding of personality types to help us relate effectively with others.

Back in the 1990s when long distance companies were competing for our telephone business, I watched the OD concept of equal peers put to the test by a friend who wanted to start his own phone company. He was a very secure person who didn't need the ego satisfaction of being the Big Boss. What he wanted was success. So he formed a company without bosses. Other people could buy into his company as equal partners who would never receive any salary; their income was based entirely on the business they brought into the company. He negotiated with an existing long-distance carrier to buy many hours of long-distance time from them at a 30 percent discounted rate. Then he sold that time to business customers at a 15 percent markup of his costs. He made 15 percent, and his customers saved 15 percent. Soon he was also leasing phone systems to his customers. Within five years, several of those partners had become millionaires, and my friend was able to sell his successful business to one of the major carriers. I think since then my friend has spent a lot of time chasing a little white ball all over a green pasture!

Asbury Seminary has always been a little bit different from Duke and Emory—more evangelical, for one thing—and therefore, ministers who were trained there are sometimes a bit different also. But in Joe's case, I grew to respect his unique insights. For one thing, Joe consistently referred to our most difficult problems in biblical terms. These were our demons! Of course, he didn't mean that literally, but since people with mental and emotional health issues were said to be possessed by "demons" in Jesus's day, Joe referred to our difficult human struggles as our demons. Alcohol does seem to possess some people, as do nicotine and certain drugs, and some of us struggle with depression, fears, anger, and anxieties most of our lives. I found it very helpful to think of these struggles as our personal "demons," and it was also very helpful to believe that Jesus was still in the business today of freeing people from these "spiritual forces of wickedness" and "evil powers of this world" via a loving faith community.

I haven't used what I learned in every training event I have taken across the years, but I have just about worn out all I learned from my friend and mentor Joe Alley.

Chapter 14

The Reverend John Rush

Greer, South Carolina, is a great place to retire as shown by the number of former pastors of Memorial United Methodist Church who retired there.

The Reverend John Rush was one of these retirees who blessed me with his continuing participation in our church after I became its pastor.

John had been the preacher there for eight years right at the turn of the millennium. I would have worn out a dozen pairs of shoes a year if I had tried to keep up with him in his pastoral care visitation. His care of members allowed me to give my time to other areas of the church that needed my attention, things like a major building program, a growing youth and children's ministry, and the inauguration of a new contemporary worship service (I even ended up singing with the excellent band).

John's other help was at almost every funeral. He knew everything about everybody, so I never had to worry about the funeral being individually tailored. John also found a paraphrase of John 14:6 that he liked better than the usual one read at funerals, and I quickly adopted that paraphrase myself: "No one comes to know God as Father except through me." John had a dry sense of humor, and he would often drop by my office whenever he found a humorous obituary—

usually a funny nickname, like a man with the last name "Pye" whose obituary was listed as "Cow Pye."

South Carolina was lucky to get the Rush brothers as United Methodist pastors. They both moved here from Mississippi because they both had been told to get out of the Mississippi Methodist Conference back in the 1960s after Jim Rush signed a letter from a group of young pastors who wanted to encourage better interracial relationships in the church. It wasn't a bad letter or a mean-spirited one, but it was very unpopular. John came to South Carolina via California, where he had found his wife Elaine, and the Rush brothers were deeply appreciated here in our state.

John and Elaine loved to travel, and they loved to arrange groups to travel with them. Early in my time at Memorial, they arranged a trip to Alaska. Part of the group left early in order to tour Vancouver, while our group planned to fly to Vancouver the day the ship departed. What we didn't plan for was a massive storm that swept across the country the day before our flight, causing it to be cancelled. As the travel agents worked on our crisis, John used the time to keep us laughing with his dry humor. His best line was that he was beginning to believe our cruise plans had been made by our Annual Conference leaders. Just before lunch, we boarded the first of a series of planes that got us to Seattle too late to make other connections that day—or any arrangements for overnight stay—and so we were "sleepless in Seattle" that night. We lost two days of the cruise, but we caught the ship in Ketchikan, Alaska. But we really hadn't lost anything because we had so much fun together.

One of John's greatest gifts was his ability to keep absolutely calm in all circumstances. I could always count of him to settle me down when my Holt blood pressure would start to rise as anger saturated my bones.

John didn't realize how funny he could be when he had an "absent-minded" moment. One night, the ship docked, and we assembled in a lobby to walk a hundred yards to the dining area. Elaine decided she wouldn't wait with the rest of us and instead headed on toward supper. She got about halfway there when the skies opened and a flash flood happened! She was closer to our lobby, and so she turned around. She was absolutely drenched—including her umbrella. I thought I would die laughing when John said to her, "Maybe you should step back outside because you are dripping on the carpet." The look on Elaine's face was a mixture of amusement and the urge to kill.

As you can imagine, if we hadn't been good friends before this cruise, we were afterward.

I just wish I could remain calm like John always did, no matter what was going on. I think my eight years there were my most enjoyable and successful of all my places of ministry, and this was largely because of John Rush.

Part 3
Stories about Church Members

Chapter 15

Moose Teter

When you are twenty-five years old and have known more failures than successes in your previous jobs, and when you are giving ministry one last chance before "abandoning ship" and moving on to some other career, you need all the encouragement and training you can get. My personal and professional needs were what had led me to accept a job at Union United Methodist Church, where I could be mentored by the Reverend Julian Lazar and the leaders at this very successful church. I hoped perhaps the Lutheran seminary nearby would help me put down some deeper theological roots that could sustain my faith in difficult times.

My primary job there was youth ministry. The church had eighty youth who were actively involved, and excellent youth counselors had been recruited by my predecessor and the church's educational director, Lynn Barnes. One couple was Bob Teter and his wife Arlene. Their two elementary school age sons Mike and Bryan—we called them the "Teter Tots"—were often at youth gatherings with their parents.

Bob was a huge man who towered over all of us. Someone hung an appropriate nickname on him because of his size: "Moose."

Moose Teter suffered from a serious loss of hearing. He was almost totally deaf in one ear and had very limited hearing in the other. His daily routine included ear drops to keep his ear infections at bay, and his hearing loss was not an asset when it came to hearing what youth were discussing at their meetings. On retreats and "lock-ins" (overnights spent with youth in our gym), Moose wasn't much help with law and order; he just removed his hearing aids and slept very well!

I am not sure what led to a conversation Moose and I had one day. Maybe I had shared some of my fears about my future as a pastor, telling him I felt very inadequate when I compared myself to others. Whatever the prelude to our conversation was, I will always be grateful for his response to me that day.

"I know I am not the best youth counselor," Moose said. "Sometimes I cannot understand what the youth say during our discussions because I just can't hear well enough. I am sure that there are better equipped youth workers in our church, but where are they? Why don't they step forward and volunteer to come on Sunday nights to be with these young people? At least I am available right now, and I'll gladly get out of the way if someone better volunteers. But I am available now and I love these kids and am happy to be here for them."

There was something very liberating and encouraging to me in what Moose said. I was in great need of training and shaping for my future ministry, and I might never be as good as some others. But I was available right now, and that availability was worth something.

I've often wondered if I was recruited by God as a second- or third-string player—believe me, I am being honest and not trying to impress you with my humility. Ministry was never easy for me. Maybe I had a chance to play in the big game because a first-string recruit was injured or otherwise unable to fulfill his or her role.

Moose's words liberated me to the point that I stopped comparing myself to others and began concentrating on what contributions I could make in the lives of those kids. I could always remove myself if and when someone better came along.

Chapter 16

Odell and Mae Bledsoe

Sometimes the telephone at the parsonage in Saluda would ring late in the evening, and usually this meant someone had died. If the call came from the Bethlehem community, Mae Bledsoe would always beat me to the home of the deceased. When I arrived, I always knew where to find Mae. She would be in the kitchen, washing the family's dishes and cleaning up because visitors would be bringing food for the family. She was always a welcome presence in those homes in these times of grief.

One such call came in on a Saturday when Penny and I had been in Saluda for six months and were about to go on a real adventure. We had purchased two tickets from Trailways Bus Lines that were good for seven days of travel to any place in the country. After years in graduate school, Penny was hungering to go on a real vacation trip—to the Rockies! We planned to leave the next day right after church, but now I had this death in the congregation to attend to.

When I arrived at the home of the elderly man who had died, his widow said, "Reverend Holt, I have already called one of our former pastors who can come lead my husband's funeral. I want you and Penny to go ahead with your planned trip."

This wasn't my usual behavior—I usually dropped personal plans for deaths.

But the family insisted they would be in good hands with their former pastor. So the next day, we left for the Rockies.

A week later, we returned. I got wind that one of Bethlehem's members was upset that we had gone ahead with our trip right after a member had died. This person was not even a member of that family. He just had the opinion that I had made the wrong decision and he was going to tell me so.

I knew to be ready for him the next Sunday. As he started his angry complaint, I heard the voice of someone who had already become a dear friend—Mae Bledsoe—coming to my defense.

"You just shut up!" Mae commanded. "It's none of your business. The family made the decision to have another pastor lead the funeral. You just shut up right now."

Soundly defeated, the angry church member walked off, licking his wounds.

Mae's husband, Odell, was a mechanic who could fix anything. Preachers usually have rather humble automobiles, and mine was an old green Ford Pinto I had bought from a friend for $400. It was dependable but old and rusty. One Sunday morning as I was driving from Gassaway Church to Bethlehem, I ran through a puddle of water and got soaked. Where had that water come from? Then I noticed I could see the road under my feet—my floorboard had rusted away! I was laughing about this when I arrived for worship at Bethlehem, and naturally I told my friends about my recent "baptism."

Odell told me to come to his house on my way home so he could see what needed to be done to fix it. When I arrived, Mae was concerned about my wet pants, and so she loaned me a pair of Odell's coveralls. They were way too short for me, and so they delighted in telling our friends at church how I looked wearing "high water britches."

The next day, I took my car to Odell, and I saw this retired man crawl under my car with a thin piece of metal that he attached to what was left of the car's frame. Then he caulked the cracks, and I was good to go. Odell didn't just know how to fix things—he got down on his hands and knees to do this work for his friends. He was often the one the church turned to when things at church broke and needed fixing.

I am always looking for things to tease folks about because laughing with someone is such a strong bonding experience. Soon after we arrived in Saluda, Mae and Odell invited us to come to their home for Sunday dinner. Odell walked over to our car to tell us that since we didn't know where they lived, we should follow their car. Apparently, Mae thought Odell was going to ride with us, so just as Odell walked up to the passenger door of their car, Mae put it in gear and took off. She just about took his arm off! Odell tried to run after the car but soon gave up and walked back to our car for a lift. I had so much fun teasing them about what had looked to me like a scene from The Three Stooges.

Odell had the ability to fall asleep whenever he sat still for any length of time—in his chair at home and at church in his pew. Mae sang in the church choir, but the choir members usually left the choir loft and sat with their families for the sermon, and I just know poor Odell always had bruises in his side from being awakened by Mae's elbow. Odell must have been at peace with his conscience to fall asleep so easily!

Every year, the three churches of the Saluda Circuit each had homecoming followed by a delicious covered-dish dinner. When weather permitted, Bethlehem's homecoming dinner was always held outside on the grounds. Cleanup of the yard would be done a few days before the dinner. Grass would be cut and limbs would be picked up. One year, I was helping with the cleanup when I stepped into a puddle of water.

"Look here," I said with excitement. "There's a spring here in the yard!"

I heard Odell chuckle before he said, "No, we just never got around to putting in a septic tank."

As I shook the water off my wet shoes, I suggested we get around to it very soon. Another man said we didn't have to put in a septic tank now because the electric power (which was supposed to be turned on only after the septic tank was installed) had been turned on already. I figured if this didn't bother these men or their wives, I could live with it.

A week or two later, the county health department paid a visit to a neighboring Baptist Church that had a similar situation—electric power on but no septic tank. That health department inspector padlocked the doors on that Baptist Church, demanding that a septic tank of a certain size and design be installed before they could use their church again. My folks heard about this and decided to install a septic tank of their choice before the inspector locked our doors and demanded that we install a more expensive one. It felt good to be an inexperienced young pastor and to be vindicated!

A pastor knows he or she has gained the trust of a church member when that member says to us, "I've never felt like I could ask a pastor this, but I feel like I could ask you." That level of trust feels so good. In Odell's case when he made this statement, he was curious about what a certain statement in the Apostles' Creed meant. He was a bit embarrassed that he didn't already know this, but he wondered why we said we believe in the "holy catholic church." Like many others, he thought we were saying that we believed the Roman Catholic Church was the right church. He was relieved when he learned just what the holy catholic church was—the invisible body of believers in all churches everywhere who believe in Jesus.

After three and a half years, I was moved twenty-two miles from downtown Saluda to downtown Edgefield. In my new parsonage, I lived just as close to Mae and Odell as I had been before, but now phone calls were not long distance. I got many phone calls from friends at Bethlehem just to check on me and tell me family news. But I also got a call from Mae, telling me Odell was not doing well. He was suffering from prostate cancer.

We have an understanding in The United Methodist Church that we pastors cut ties when we move to a new assignment. This is a bit painful to us, but it is necessary if our successor is going to be accepted as the pastor of that church. So I contacted the new pastor to explain my closeness to Mae and Odell, and he graciously invited me to not worry about overstepping any boundaries. He was also aware of the seriousness of Odell's illness. So I made several visits to his home, but in a very short time Odell died, and I lost a dear friend.

Mae lived about twenty-five years after Odell died. For quite a while, she continued her vital ministry in her church and community and enjoying her children and grandchildren. After I moved away from that area, Mae began losing her balance and falling. I believe she also had Parkinson's disease. She moved into the Saluda Nursing and Rehab Center and started using a wheelchair and wearing a helmet for protection. I would go by to see her whenever I was in that area because our friendship was very special to me.

It isn't every day that pastors have a person come to their defense saying, "You just shut up!"

Chapter 17

Mrs. Kate

There were eight United Methodist churches in Saluda, South Carolina, in the 1980s. Three of them on the Butler Circuit shared one pastor. The large church near Lake Murray and the big church in downtown Saluda each had their own pastor. The other three were on the Saluda Circuit that I was appointed to in 1981. I drove thirty miles each Sunday to preach at each of those three churches. I was only thirty-one, but I needed a nap every Sunday afternoon.

There also were churches of other denominations in Saluda County, and every one of them had members who lived at the Saluda Nursing and Rehab Center because of their poor health. Some of those residents were quite colorful—like Big Boy DeLoach, whose fondness for strong drink caused him to run away from the nursing home to his old shack about once a year. But he always returned to the nursing home when he ran out of refreshments.

I enjoyed talking with Big Boy and other residents, but my purpose for going to the nursing center usually was to see my own members, like Mrs. Kate Rushton. Mrs. Kate was born in 1892, and she was eighty-nine when we first met. She had lost both legs because of complications from diabetes, but that didn't keep her from going all over the nursing center in her wheelchair.

I would catch up with her as she was speeding down the hall and ask, "Mrs. Kate, where in the world are you going so fast?"

She would always say, "Wherever I please!"

If I found her sitting out near the nurses' station and asked her what she was doing, her answer was always, "I am doing whatever I please!"

When she wanted to make me laugh, she would make up a story, like the time she told me she was on her way to the nurse's office to have her toenails clipped (back up a few paragraphs if you don't see her humor!). She was as well adjusted to living away from her home as anyone I've ever met in nursing facilities, and that says a lot about her faith. Of course, having her two sons and two daughters plus grandchildren visit her every day probably had a lot to do with her happy adjustment.

But one of the first things I learned about her was that she had known much sorrow in her life. Her fifth child, another daughter, had been killed in a terrible wreck along with her husband, and this wreck had occurred very soon after their marriage. To have gone from the joy of a wedding to the sadness of two funerals in a matter of a few weeks had to be more painful than most of us ever have to endure. But Mrs. Kate faced sad events with her deep faith.

In the spring of 1982, Penny and I were expecting our first child. Naturally, we had some anxiety before the baby was born. Mentally and physically healthy babies are not guaranteed, and we were both older than most first-time parents. I mentioned our anxiety to Mrs. Kate one day, and she told me that seventy years earlier when she and her husband were starting a family, their first three babies died shortly after their births.

"How did you survive these losses?" I asked her.

She shrugged her shoulders and reminded me that infant mortality had been very high in those days. It wasn't out of the ordinary back them.

"My husband said to me, 'Don't you cry. I'm not going to cry either.'"

Together they helped each other look to the future.

Mrs. Kate also entertained me with memories of her childhood. There was one story she told me about how she and her sister had disobeyed their parents and were scolded and punished. They felt very bad about their disobedience, so Mrs. Kate asked her sister if she thought God could ever forgive them. Her sister replied, "I expect that he will. After all, I've forgiven him enough times!"

Oh, to have the wisdom of children!

After I got to know this saintly woman, it was no surprise to me that all of her children were active in Bethlehem United Methodist Church, and her grandchildren and great-grandchildren were also. Her faith was contagious and inspirational.

Chapter 18

Bob and Barbara Kay

Back in the 1950s when the Greenville District was considering where to plant new Methodist churches, there was a dirt road that marked the expected outer limits of Greenville. "Greenville will never grow beyond that dirt road," people said. As houses were built out Wade Hampton Boulevard, and as more houses were built on East North Street, the Methodist District Committee on Church Location decided on a spot near Bob Jones University to build Francis Asbury Methodist Church. It grew very fast, growing to several hundred members in just a few years.

Then somebody decided to pave that dirt road. It became the "291 Bypass," otherwise known as Pleasantburg Drive, and soon Greenville did indeed move out past it. Another new Methodist church, Aldersgate, was built in that newly opened area, and the growth at Francis Asbury stopped as quickly as it had started. About the time "United" became a part of its name, decline was already under way.

As the 1980s arrived, desperation began to set in. Many members had moved to the other side of the formerly dirt road, but there was still a dedicated group of leaders who refused to let Francis Asbury United Methodist Church die. The church's Pastor-Parish Relations Committee (the personnel committee of the church) asked District Superintendent George Duffie to appoint a young pastor with small children to their church. Duffie told them that young pastors right out of seminary were paid much less than they paid their pastor, and therefore, there was no way to appoint a young pastor to their church. Someone on the PPRC wondered what would happen if they cut the salary down to the level of most younger pastors, and they were told they couldn't do that ... but they did.

It just so happened that they set the salary a bit higher than what I was making in Edgefield, and I was moved there in June 1987, after just three years in Edgefield. It was quite a step up for me, and it was a desperate hope for the members of Francis Asbury. I certainly did not save the church, but we had some successes that brought in new members and revitalized the church for a while, anyway.

Barbara Kay was the chair of the PPRC that took such daring action. She was an executive with BellSouth, the telecommunications company. Her husband, Bob, also an employee of BellSouth, was the church's lay leader.

I probably would not have survived had it not been for those two friends. There had been a lot of conflict between the church and several pastors in recent years, and Barbara told me not to try to resolve any problems without first talking to her. She would handle the problems for me if she could. Bob is a natural salesman, and his warm welcome to visitors every Sunday was much appreciated. Bob and I met each week for coffee with some of his telephone friends, and he really encouraged my ministry.

One thing you have to know about Bob and Barbara is that they love the University of South Carolina Gamecocks football almost as much as they love their church. They went to most of the home football games and some of the away games as well. But they were always in church the next day, win or lose. Something you also must know is there is only one game each year that really matters, and that is the game between Carolina and Clemson. The membership of our church was equally divided between those two schools, and both sides were full of rabid fans. Carolina fans rooted for two teams each Saturday—the Gamecocks and whoever was playing against the

Tigers. The same was true of Clemson fans. It was an especially good Saturday for them when their team won and the other lost.

In January 1990, Bob had some chest pains. He was only in his early fifties, but it was discovered that he had some badly blocked arteries near his heart. Most of the Kay men died before their fiftieth birthday, so surgery was scheduled immediately for Bob. As Barbara and I sat in the surgery waiting room during Bob's surgery, breaking news on TV announced that Clemson's Coach Danny Ford had resigned under pressure. Ford had won a national championship in 1981, so his resignation sent shock waves all across South Carolina.

Meanwhile, Bob came through his surgery just fine. But the next day as he was waking up from anesthesia, Bob became more and more agitated. He couldn't say anything because he still had the breathing tube down his throat.

Barbara was very concerned. What could be wrong with Bob, she wondered. I went to the hospital to be with Barbara during this new crisis. Finally, the nurse came to the waiting room to tell us the breathing tube had been removed and we could go in to visit Bob.

But he still looked agitated and angry as he said to us, "Why didn't you tell me that Danny Ford had resigned?"

We had a good laugh at the man who worried more about his football team than he did his heart surgery.

One of the duties of the PPRC was to conduct annual reviews of the parsonage to make sure it wasn't being abused by the pastor and his family. Barbara would always be the inspector, and we always appreciated her understanding. Hillary was five and John was two years old when we moved to Greenville, and while we didn't abuse the parsonage, it rarely was in good enough shape for visitors or inspectors. Usually we didn't get the children's rooms in "ship shape" until the day of the visit. Of course, we wanted Barbara to believe the children's rooms were always kept as neatly as they were on the day of her visit, but once Hillary gave away our secret when she showed Barbara her room and said, "Look! I can step here and I can step here and I can step here without stepping on anything."

Chapter 19

Dinty Moore

At Francis Asbury United Methodist Church there was a man named E. M. Moore who called himself "Dinty Moore, just like the beef stew." He was another retiree from Ma Bell who joined Bob Kay and others each week for coffee at the Eckerd's Drug Store café. Dinty taught Sunday school and served on the church administrative board, and he really got stirred up about the loss of members in The United Methodist Church in general and our church in particular. He was very sure these losses were because of the "liberal policies" our denominational leaders had been following in recent years.

Dinty was not entirely wrong. We lost a number of members because of our correct stand on racial integration, and that was seen as a liberal issue back in those days. Until 1972, United Methodists in South Carolina were racially segregated into two annual conferences, but that year we merged the two conferences into one integrated conference. This meant that African-American pastors would be appointed as district superintendents of historically all-White churches, and it opened the door for a Black person to be appointed as our bishop. There were even some discussions about the possibility of cross-racial appointments—the assigning of White pastors to Black churches and vice versa—and this didn't sit well with some of our more conservative members. Many of them left The United Methodist Church for churches that used the "congregational style" of polity and could (and did) allow only White people into their church membership. If our membership loss was because of a decision to love all of God's children, I would be very proud of that fact.

Another issue that concerned many people in those days was the fact that while we still deployed missionaries all over the world via the Board of Global Ministries, very few of them were traditional missionaries that made converts and established churches. In the mid-1980s, a group of conservative leaders in our denomination decided there needed to be a second missionary arm to correct this deficiency. The Mission Society for United Methodists was created as an unofficial missionary deployment program, and leaders in our denomination were afraid the Mission Society would siphon off some funds that normally went to support the work of Global Ministries. However, Dinty was all in favor of this new Mission Society, and he wanted our church to support it—even if it meant diverting some Global Ministry funds.

Apportionments are a big deal in The United Methodist Church, and I always advocated for 100 percent payment from the church I served. It wasn't because of pressure from my district superintendent or bishop (although that was always present). For me, it was the fact that our denomination's form of polity makes us a "representative democracy." Each local church sends delegates to our Annual Conference, where delegates to Jurisdictional and General conferences are elected. Those who we elect decide on budget items for the entire denomination. For a local church to decide they will not pay their portion of what their elected delegates passed always seemed to me to be a disloyal action. In theory, Dinty agreed with this understanding of apportionments and was not at all difficult to get along with. But he was as adamant about our church supporting the Mission Society as I was about supporting Global Ministries.

Peggy Bridges, a retired schoolteacher, was our administrative board chair, and she was afraid we were headed for a churchwide blow up. Therefore, she laid down the law at our administrative board meeting, urging us to behave like adult Christians who respected each other. She said those who got out of line would be asked to leave the meeting. Even her husband, "Paul the Bald," seemed a bit shocked by Peggy's authoritative approach, but we all respected Peggy and knew she meant it. From time to time, Peggy reminded us that her ancestors were Vikings!

But what Peggy didn't know was that Dinty and I had been negotiating over coffee. Henry Kissinger would have been proud of us. We had come to an agreement that I would not oppose putting several thousand dollars in our budget for the Mission Society and that Dinty would not oppose our full support of our apportionments. We could do both. It was a win-win situation for us and for our church.

That was the good old United Methodist Church that I always appreciated. I love it when people find a way to get along!

While I was at Francis Asbury UMC, the calendar rolled over on me and hit me with my fortieth birthday. The church decided to "roast" me at a surprise birthday party, and Dinty was one of the roasters. He had some great lines—like, "When Arthur was born, the doctor gave him a funny look. He still has it!" Just as funny was his statement, "People used to say that whoever Arthur married would have to be able to take a joke, and Penny is the only girl who would take him."

I was away from the area for most of the 1990s, but I was in Spartanburg for the early 2000s. That's when I received word that Dinty was in a nursing home and would love to see me.

I had several good visits with my old, dear friend Dinty before he joined the Church Triumphant.

Chapter 20

John I. Warner Jr.

Several members of Francis Asbury United Methodist Church felt like they had to warn me about one of the members, who had a reputation of dropping by the church just to see if the preacher was on the job or not. I was almost always in the office from 9:00 a.m. to noon, so I wasn't worried about an auditor. And after a few times of talking with John I. Warner Jr., I decided those who'd "warned" me about "Warner" were mistaken about him. I saw him to be someone whose sense of humor was often misunderstood, so I decided to proceed with that assumption and respond accordingly.

It turned out I was right, thank goodness. John might growl like a bear, but he was a teddy bear. He enjoyed playful kidding as much as I do. I soon had a dear friend who had fun picking on me and being picked on by me. It seemed to me the members of the church gave a collective sigh of relief after they saw their fears had been diffused.

I remember his first "complaint." I usually read three Scripture passages in worship and then preach on one of them. After my first sermon, John told me that if I was going to read that much from the Bible each week, we would never beat the Baptists to the restaurants. I replied that his wife told me he could stand to miss a meal or two and that if anybody needed to hear more of the Bible read in church, surely it was him!

We all could tell he loved the attention I gave him.

Francis Asbury church was struggling to survive, but they were also very involved in mission causes in Greenville. Offerings were collected for the food distribution service of United Ministries. John began talking with the managers of area grocery stores, asking them to let him purchase slightly out-of-date boxes of mac and cheese at a big discount. They agreed, and soon we were turning those donations over to John to use in his deals for the needy. It was amazing to see United Ministries' shelves fully stocked by the gifts of our church and the work of John Warner. John gave us such a good reputation in the community as a church that could be depended on to feed hungry families.

John loved the Big Band sound of the 1940s. Once he heard me telling someone I knew a great deal about automobile stereos and had installed several new radios in different cars I'd owned. John was not happy with his radio, as it had way too much static. I told him several things to try before he bought a new stereo, like buying higher-quality spark plugs and wires and an inline noise filter. He called me after getting all that done by a professional mechanic. When the mechanic reconnected his battery, it blew all of the fuses in his car! I never heard the end of this as he enjoyed telling church friends that I, a self-proclaimed expert in car radios, had caused him to spend $500 without fixing his problem. Sometime after that, his son and I gave in and installed a new high-dollar stereo radio and tape player in his old car.

John also had a heart of gold when it came to helping people out. Penny and I had two preschool children and two old cars. The family car, a Buick station wagon, was in need of an air conditioning compressor, but we were always too broke to consider this. So John paid for this repair. He said he loved John and Hillary, and especially Penny, and he wanted them to be cool during the summer.

As for me, I could burn up—in the car and also in the life to come!

Chapter 21

Memorable Baptisms

Here in the South, we live in a culture that seems to believe an adult "believer's baptism" is the only correct way to baptize a person. But the fact is that the holy universal church has been baptizing babies of believers from the earliest days of the church, and the practice was never questioned until the Middle Ages. Infant baptism clearly fulfills the Scripture that says, "While we were still sinners, Christ died for us" (Romans 5:8 NIV). Before a baby can possibly have personal faith or understanding of the significance of baptism, we declare the baby to be already loved and redeemed by God. For us, the emphasis is on God's action instead of human decisions, and that is what makes baptism a sacrament for us.

Every baptism is special, but several stand out in my memory. One time a toddler responded to my hand on her head by reaching her tiny hand out and touching the top of my head. It looked like we were baptizing each other!

But the baptism of twins in Rock Hill was unforgettable. The Reid family assembled at Mount Holly United Methodist Church one beautiful Sunday morning to witness the baptism of their two boys. The first infant was baptized without incident, but the second boy provided his own fanfare. After a diaper desecration that was heard in every corner of that church, this little boy was smiling happily as I took him from his parents. There was very little solemnity left in this house of worship after that, as you can imagine.

After a prayer for the boys and their family, I returned to the pulpit, aware that we had all just witnessed a parable I had to share with the congregation. The way that second baby was presented to God is the way we all come to God—with our best righteousness looking like filthy rags in comparison to the righteousness of our perfect God. We come just as we are, dirty diapers and all, and God in God's grace accepts us just as we are because of God's gracious love.

This little boy experienced that, even if he didn't understand it.

Chapter 22

Bill Gibbons

I was his interim pastor for only one year, but in that year Bill Gibbons and I became close friends. There are several ways a person and his pastor become good friends, and the least popular but very common way is during a serious illness. As we all were getting ready for Thanksgiving in 2018, my ninety-year-old friend was rushed to Spartanburg Regional Hospital with a heart attack.

Bill's doctors told the family that without heart bypass surgery, Bill had only weeks to live. But such surgery would be very serious at his age.

To my surprise, Bill didn't hesitate one minute. He told his doctors and all of us that he would take the risk of surgery because there were still some things he wanted to accomplish. I joined the family in supporting Bill's decision, but he had already done so much for his Gaffney community. After all, the "Gaffney Strangler" would never have been captured without Bill's help.

A half-century ago, back when I was about to graduate from high school, a thirty-two-year-old woman was found dead by strangulation. Her husband was tried and convicted of her murder. The community was relieved when this murder seemed to be solved, but one man was not relieved. He had gotten away with that murder and now felt like he had something to prove. In February 1968, two young women were kidnapped. One was a twenty-year-old young wife, and the other was a fourteen-year-old teenage girl.

Word spread all over the Upstate that there was a serial kidnapper in Gaffney. Even twenty miles away in my hometown of Spartanburg, the fear was intense. What if the kidnapper ventured over to our town? The young lady who would be my bride in three years was a freshman at Converse College, and she remembers how the college girls walked in large groups on campus for protection. Nobody had any leads on who the kidnapper was, and the kidnapped girls had not been found.

The inability of law officers to find the latest two victims caused the kidnapper to reach out to the editor of the *Gaffney Ledger* newspaper, Bill Gibbons. The kidnapper phoned Bill anonymously, claiming the husband who had been convicted of killing his wife was innocent and that he—the caller—was the actual killer. He then told Bill where the bodies of the two recently kidnapped girls could be found.

Bill called the police, and the two bodies were found exactly where the anonymous caller had said they would be. Each had been assaulted and strangled.

Now Upstate citizens were terrified. There was a serial killer living in Gaffney. Newspapers and television news reported on the "Gaffney Strangler" every day. In Gaffney, there were some citizens who thought it odd that one man seemed to know a lot about the strangler. Some went so far as to say that the reason Bill knew so much was because he was the strangler! Bill, his wife, Tedi, and their two young children were the victims of slander, gossip, and fear.

Four days after the bodies of the two victims had been found, the Gaffney Strangler called Bill at the newspaper office again. The caller warned that there would be more murders in the future. This time, a police tap on Bill's phone allowed the authorities to listen in on the conversation between Bill and the caller; the next time someone raised the concern that Bill might be the strangler, the police were able to say they witnessed Bill talking with the strangler and this should be enough to stop that suspicion.

The next day, a fifteen-year-old girl was abducted as she walked toward a school bus stop with her sister. Her sister was able to describe the kidnapper's car to the police, and this would lead to an arrest. Volunteers drove around the county, looking for a car matching the description.

Two men drove by a car that was backed down a dirt road in a wooded area, and the driver drove off very quickly. But they were able to get his license number. Investigators went to that location and found the body of the Gaffney Strangler's last victim, and the car license plate led to the arrest of Lee Roy Martin.

At last, the citizens could see Bill Gibbons as the hero who had helped solve these crimes.

After Martin's arrest, people began telling stories about how they worked in the mill with him and never would have believed he could be the killer. One woman always asked Martin to walk her to her car when they got off work so she would be safe! Bill and his family returned to normal life, being active in Buford Street United Methodist Church.

And that is where I got to know this real-life hero I had learned about fifty years ago.

Bill did recover from his heart bypass surgery and returned to his active participation in his community. But he and Tedi decided it was in their best interest to move closer to Gaffney from way out in the country. Their land and beautiful house were sold to someone who planned to open a tree farm and nursery on the site.

By now it was spring, and my time as interim pastor was coming to a close. But I made time to help them carry boxes out of their old house, load them into a truck, and then unload those boxes at their new house in town. This was a labor of love and respect for them both. Besides, if an itinerant pastor knows anything, he or she knows all about packing boxes and moving!

At their new home, Bill was having trouble getting his washer hooked up to water lines. He needed a young man to climb over the washer, make the connections, and then climb back out. But since no young man could be found, I crawled back behind the washer. I had a very difficult time climbing back out of that tiny space, and Bill told everybody how funny I looked, trapped in his kitchen.

Tedi had a stroke, and this beloved former schoolteacher and church choir member died a few months later. Less than a year later, I learned that Bill was back in the Spartanburg hospital. He slept through my first visit, but after he was moved to a rehab center, we had a good visit. He was moved again, this time to a long-term care facility, and I promised his family I would visit with him there very soon. But I have a busy life and an absent mind, and I let several weeks go by before I got a strange reminder that I honestly believe was a "God thing."

As I was driving through Spartanburg, a car with the name of that rehab facility written on its side shot by me on my left and then slowed down once it was in front of me. I turned my car around and headed in Bill's direction, and our visit that day was absolutely wonderful. He seemed like his old self again. I was full of hope for many more good visits, but he died a few days later. If I had not received the reminder from that speeding car, I would have missed out on this wonderful final visit with my friend.

At his funeral, stories of his service to his community were shared, and I learned that Bill had done so much for the youth of Gaffney. As a newspaper writer and radio broadcaster, Bill was often asked to be the emcee at youth dances. One speaker mentioned how he had met his wife at one of these events and wanted to thank Bill for his influence.

And I had to remember that ninety-year-old friend who knelt with a group of us every Wednesday morning to pray for our church and community, a man who still drove his truck and took other members of that prayer group home each week, and a man who answered the church phone one day each week as he addressed cards and letters to church members. Some people keep on living and giving until it is time for them to go "home."

Chapter 23

Practical Jokesters

I grew up in a wonderful extended family that valued laughter almost as much as they did faith. No one ever told a joke that would hurt someone's feelings; what we said and did had a way of affirming the other persons. Across the years of my life and ministry, I have found that loving jokes told on people brought them and me closer together.

Of course, if you are going to dish it out, you'd better be able to also take it.

One of my first district superintendents was Chad Davis, and he took special interest in all of the young seminarians who were also working in churches in the Columbia District. He was a big kidder and he loved the fact that I would return his kidding with barbs of my own.

One of the jokes making the rounds in the 1970s was how it seemed our male bishops always appointed male district superintendents that were similar in outward appearance. At one gathering of pastors, I called everyone's attention to this fact saying, "When Paul Hardin was our bishop, he picked men of small stature like Joel Cannon. When Bishop Roy Clark was here, he selected tall, thin men like Jack Meadors and George Duffie Jr. But when heavyset bishop Tullis was our bishop, he chose similarly sized men like Peden Gene

Curry, Bill Kinnett, and Chad Davis to be on his cabinet."

Chad didn't miss a beat. His reply was, "And Arthur, if we ever get an ugly redhead bishop, your day will have come."

Chapter 24

A Kidding Custodian

One of the first things we did right after I arrived in Greenville at Francis Asbury United Methodist Church in 1987 was start repairing our old gym so it would be ready for use in the Methodist Basketball League. The basketball league had been very meaningful to the church in past years. We saw it as a means of recruiting children and youth and new members, but the gym had been neglected for several years. There was torn plastic insulation on the walls, and we made plans to cover the ugly walls with metal siding. It also had fluorescent tube lights hanging down on long chains from the very high ceiling, and most of those of tubes were either dead or in need of replacement.

Our part-time custodian Bob Putnam said he would be glad to help me change those tubes, but he was afraid of climbing up an A-frame ladder with an extension. It was just too high, he said. But he would hold the ladder for me if I would climb it.

I was in my thirties back then,—I could do this, I told myself. So I held a florescent tube in one hand and held on with the other as I climbed up about twenty-five feet toward the light fixture.

Bob told me how he had seen others replace those tube lights. They would secure themselves on the ladder by twisting their legs and feet around the ladder in such a way that would make it impossible for them to fall. But try as I might, I never felt that secure up there, so I tried to change the tube with one hand while holding onto the ladder with the other hand.

I just couldn't do it.

I was about to give up when a church member, Jim Burgin, came into the gym.

"Preacher, what are you doing way up there on that ladder?" he asked.

I explained that the florescent lights needed to be fixed and that Bob was afraid of heights.

Jim began laughing, and then he said, "Bob Putnam is the assistant fire chief of the Greenville City Fire Department. He climbs ladders taller than that all the time! Get down from there."

I was ready to comply with his wishes.

Then I saw Jim scamper up that ladder (Bob was laughing too hard to do it), and I saw how Jim twisted his legs and feet around that ladder so tightly he was able to turn loose and use both hands to fix the lights.

And I learned to always second-guess our part-time custodian Bob Putnam—who was really the assistant fire chief of the city. We were going to have a good time kidding each other.

Chapter 25

Find the Crazies

"Just as soon as you move into a new community, find the place where the crazies gather and join them." This advice from my friend Phil Lavender may have been the most valuable I ever received.

Parish ministry is such serious business that most of us pastors need a place to gather just for laughs. Such groups just might keep your brain from imploding.

For several years I lived in a Southern county-seat town. Politics was serious business there. Racially segregated high schools were merging. The activity most of the men did for relaxation was golf, but it also seemed to be serious business to those guys. Lots of them also hunted—mostly for deer—and there seemed to be a fair amount of competition between the citizens of the county over how successful you had been on your latest hunting trip.

But a group of men met around coffee and breakfast at a local restaurant on Monday through Friday of each week. The unwritten rule at these morning gatherings was that everything had to be kept lighthearted and friendly.

Whenever someone came in saying, "I got my first deer of the season," someone was bound to ask him how badly his car had been damaged. Sometimes that was true! One man said his wife wanted to go hunting with him, so he set her up in a deer stand by a dirt road where she was unlikely to see any wildlife. But he had barely gotten to his deer stand before he heard his wife's rifle fire. As he ran back to her position, he heard the voice of a man saying, "OK, lady. It's a deer and it's yours! Do you mind if I get my saddle off it?"

Many days I found a better mental outlook for the day ahead after meeting with those good men.

In my last two communities, I found the crazies were gathering for breakfast at local Waffle Houses. But that's not the reason I went back after the first visit. I was fascinated by the language spoken between waitstaff and the cooks. It is a study in how language evolved in communities based on the need to say a lot in as few words as possible, and in the case of Waffle House, it means the cooks never read the written orders. Instead, they mark each plate with condiments in corners or sides, and those markings help them remember the orders. As the orders are called out by the staff, cooks are reminded to "mark" the plate, "drop" the hashbrowns, and "pull" the meat. One of the things I am convinced of is that I am not smart enough to learn a new language and go to work at a Waffle House!

At one Waffle House, my usual waitress was missing one day, and her coworker told me a sad story about her. She had not been able to complete her education because her mother had gotten sick, and she had dropped out to help raise her younger siblings. But now she had enrolled in adult education, and that would mean she wouldn't be at work every day. It made perfect sense to me, especially after that coworker reminded me about her very poor handwriting on my breakfast bills.

So the next week when she returned, I started leaving her bigger tips. After a few more weeks, I asked her how her classes were going.

She cocked her head in the direction of her coworker, who laughed and then ran into the back. Then she asked me, "Did she tell you I dropped out of high school before I graduated and that I am enrolled in adult education?"

I shyly replied, "Yes."

She started laughing, as did her coworker in the back. Apparently I was not the first customer to be taken in by this tall tale. But that made me want to go back every day to catch up on their craziness, and I really grew to appreciate those two ladies.

In my retirement years, I found the crazies were gathering for breakfast at a local Waffle House near my new home. Every Waffle House has its regulars, and so I started sitting at the high counter with them. They were always kidding with each other and with several of the waitresses, and those ladies could dish it out as easily as they received it. So one day I decided to venture into the fray. After my coffee cup had been ignored for a short while, I said very loudly to another customer, "Is the coffee good today? You see, I wouldn't know because I haven't had any coffee lately." I almost got coffee poured in my lap that day. But I had joined the club!

Soon after this, I earned a reputation for being a troublemaker, so Doris, one of the waitstaff, decided she didn't want to look at me that day. She took five or six laminated menus and built a wall around my counter space. The other customers seemed to enjoy the show.

Here is the unexpected benefit of finding a group of crazies. You actually make some dear friends. I took an interim pastor job in another town thirty miles away. On my first and my last Sundays there, I looked up to see my friend Doris at the church—and this was in spite of the fact that she loves to tell everybody she fell asleep the first time she ever heard me speak.

Often now when I go for breakfast, Doris will yell out, "I hope everybody is prayed up because the devil just came into the house," and then she will refer to me as "Lucifer." It is Olivia's job to send me out with this blessing: "Satan, I cast thee out."

Someone asked me how I felt about being called "Satan," and I said, "If Jesus could call his best friend Simon Peter 'Satan,' I guess it is okay for me, too."

So this is the house of crazies that keeps me going. If you are very lucky, you will find a similar place where the crazies gather. They will keep you from taking life much too seriously.

Part 4
Things I Wrote for Facebook

Chapter 26

I Know I Am a Little Different

I know that as a person of faith, I am a little different ... not better. Just different.

Some of my friends were baptized as children as a way of confirming their commitment to Christ. I was baptized as an infant as a way of affirming Christ's commitment to me.

While some folks were memorizing the Ten Commandments, we were learning how to apply the Beatitudes (the Be-Like-Jesus-Attitudes).

While some were learning Old Testament stories, my church was teaching me about Jesus, about being a good Samaritan and a peacemaker, and that "Jesus loves the little children ... red and yellow, black and white, they are special in his sight."

I didn't grow up fearing hell or believing that Jesus saved me from hell; I was taught that Jesus had saved me for God's purpose—to use me as his servant in this life.

I grew to really appreciate the Bible, but my loyalty was never to a book but rather to a person. I look to Jesus for my guidance.

I also loved the creeds and confessions and enjoyed learning about Christian doctrines, but my primary loyalty has never been to them. They point me to the truth, but they are not the truth.

As a young adult, I once again heard the call of Jesus: "Follow me."

I was not called to teach a book but to teach the way of life that Jesus demonstrated. I haven't always been successful.

I knew Jesus often found himself disagreeing with others about how to interpret the Bible correctly, so I have always expected there would be some occasions in my life when Jesus would lead me to believe or act in ways that seemed to contradict the words of scripture.

I learned that love, grace, and forgiveness were God's characteristics and that these needed to be my character traits as well.

Chapter 27

Are You Watching Me, Jesus?

There's a camera at the day care my grandchild attends.
I can watch her on the playground as she plays with her friends.
I see her as she rides a trike and as she comes down the slide
And playing with some blocks when she comes back inside.

Are you watching me, Jesus?

I'd really rather be there with her, but I can't be there today.
At least this camera visit provides me one more way
To feel a little closer to one I love so dear,
And feel our deep connection when I cannot be right there.

Are you watching me, Jesus?

It is a very good thing that she is there, learning all alone.
Without me hovering over her, she'll do things on her own.
She will learn independence as I watch from that camera above.
All she needs from me is the assurance of my unfailing love.

Are you watching me, Jesus?

Chapter 28

The God I Believe in Never Changes

God never changes. God loves us and never stops loving us.

God did not design salvation to be like an Easter egg hunt where only the people who find the one right egg get to go to heaven and the rest of us are left out. Our heavenly Father wants all his children to live eternally with him, and that is what Christmas and Easter are all about.

The need to learn about God is a God-given instinct in everyone, and all religions are human attempts to understand God. The Bible says that from one man God created all the nations so they would seek God and perhaps reach out and find God (Acts 17).

God did not try to trick us by hiding dinosaur bones in the ground to see if we would believe science or Genesis 1.

God is the author of all truth, even truth that comes from science.

God did not stop revealing new truths after the Bible was written and assembled. Jesus said, "I have much more to say to you, more than you can now bear. But when he, the Spirit of truth, comes, he will guide you into all the truth."

Chapter 29

Diversity

I am becoming more and more thankful for the role that diversity has played in my life and my faith development.

Having grown up in the old segregated South, I am thankful Mom chose to shop for groceries at one of Daddy's customer's stores, even though it was way across town. Usually we were the only White customers in the store, and we were always treated with kindness.

Having grown up all my life in one Methodist church, I am thankful my faith got challenged by my Calvinist wife, by charismatic friends, by Lutheran seminary professors and students, and by my United Methodist ministerial colleagues who often didn't see eye-to-eye with me. These folks caused me to enlarge my understanding of faith and opened up new ways of seeing the truth.

Finally, I am thankful for the love and trust I have received from lesbian, gay, bisexual, transgender, and questioning/queer persons who have shared their stories with me, allowing me to learn about their struggles for self-understanding and acceptance. Their deep commitment to their faith in Christ is deeper than mine will ever be and has cost them more than my faith will ever demand of me.

So my word to you today is "diversity." Get to know some people who are not like you. They will enrich your life and your faith.

Chapter 30

The United Methodist Church

I've been a United Methodist my entire life, although I've explored many options. One of the things I have found attractive about our tradition is its openness to allowing its members to have different points of view on many doctrines and practices. This grew out of John Wesley's "Catholic (Universal) Spirit." For him, it was enough to know that our hearts agreed we had peace with God through Christ. On all else, we could disagree.

This was so helpful to me during my early adult years when nobody knew where my theology would land. I was like a fly at a picnic in those days. At a time when I was quite conservative, I found that my church was open to my perspective, but they also expected me to be open to other perspectives. This was the perfect spiritual atmosphere for me to explore and grow in my faith, and it is undoubtedly the reason for my theological journey toward the liberal side of the faith in recent years.

But I quickly discovered that some United Methodists were not happy with this openness. New groups formed to advance particular points of view. The Good News group came along in the 1960s to make sure we did not neglect making disciples at a time when we were so active in the social issues of our day.

A more conservative group, The Confessing Movement, came

along later as an attempt to write a basic confession of beliefs that all United Methodists could agree upon. One year this group asked all churches to vote on their confession, and this vote was ruled "out of order" by our district superintendents and bishops, who reminded us that only our General Conference had the authority to state what we believe (and this had not changed since before the birth of the church).

Then the Wesleyan Covenant Association, arguably the most conservative faction, came along a few years ago, hoping to move us toward strict Bible beliefs and away from tradition, experience, and reason. These movements led to the creation of the new Global Methodist Church in 2022 because they (especially the WCA) saw they were not going to be successful in their attempt to remake The United Methodist Church in their likeness or to force the centrists and liberals to change our stand on the full inclusion of LGBTQ+ persons.

Most of the churches that have disaffiliated have decided to remain independent and not belong to any denomination, which I find interesting. But in a year or so, after the dust settles, there will be two major Methodist denominations in the world, one that will be very conservative and uniform, guided primarily by the scriptures, and the other that will still be defined by openness to various ideas, still looking to the Wesleyan Quadrilateral that balances tradition, scripture, experience, and reason.

I'm sticking with the one that has faithfully nurtured me all my life.

Chapter 31

A Lesson from Acts 10

I am well aware that there are many differences between the biblical story in Acts 10 and the conflict in The United Methodist Church today. But there are enough similarities to offer us a bit of guidance. Both Acts 10 and today's issue deal with who is to be granted full inclusion in the church and under what conditions.

In the beginning of the church, all members were Hebrew. If you were a member of the Jewish race and religion and you believed that Jesus was the Messiah, you met all the conditions for inclusion in the Christian Church.

But if you were of a different race and religion—with different religion being the most important—you could not immediately join the church. First, you had to give up your old religion and become a member of the Judaic faith. For males, this meant you had to be circumcised and follow all of the strict Hebrew dietary laws. You were expected to honor Hebrew holy days. You were also expected to conform to the Hebrew laws and commandments, including tithing. If you were not in right standing with the Hebrew covenant, it really didn't matter if you already believed in Christ. You had to leave your old ways behind you and become a righteous Jew.

The early church was evenly divided between those who concurred what I just wrote and those who disagreed and thought it was enough for the Gentiles to believe in Christ. James, another son of Mary and Joseph, led this Hebrew faction while former Pharisee Paul of Tarsus led the more lenient group. Simon Peter was caught in the middle, and even though he was the one who carried the Christian faith to Cornelius and the Gentiles, he was torn between the two factions.

If you read the Book of Acts and the letters of Paul, Peter, and James, you will see just how contentious this division was. This disagreement caused Paul to be thrown in jail several times, and Peter was known to act like the Gentiles and enjoy their unkosher food unless the Hebrew faction was also there. When the Hebrew Christians were around, Peter acted like he didn't know those Gentile Christians—or else he acted like they were second-class Christians.

Before the end of the first century, Paul's faction had won the debate, and this resulted in great success in recruiting Gentiles into the church and total failure to make new Jewish disciples. The church was primarily a Gentile organization by the second century.

There is a fascinating statement made by the apostle Paul in Acts 17.

Paul was in Athens, waiting to be joined by his fellow missionaries. He began conversations about Christianity with the Jews in the synagogue, and he eventually started conversations in the marketplace with the Greeks.

Since the Greeks enjoyed hearing new ideas and new philosophies, they invited Paul to a meeting and asked him to explain his faith to them. In his brief talk, Paul told them he believed that God is the creator of heaven and earth, that God doesn't live in temples or idols but that we live in God, and that Jesus is the Christ whom God raised from death.

But here is what I find to be a very interesting statement from Paul. He said that God made all the various human families (nations) from one man and set the boundaries for their lands—both geographically and historically—so each nation would seek God and perhaps reach out and find God. And then Paul adds that this is possible because God is "not far from any one of us" (Acts 17:26-27).

I am aware that countless religions have been born in various places all around the globe, and I know the members of each religion insist that their faith is the only right one. But since Paul tells us God established our separate races and nations for the purpose of encouraging all nations to seek God, shouldn't we have at least a little respect for those other religions that came from those searches? If God established the process that led people to realize God's love and nearness to all of God's children, shouldn't we—out of respect for God—try to respect each other's faith?

And isn't it possible to hold firmly to what we each believe and still respect what others believe?

Chapter 32

My Simple Tract

1. Your Heavenly Father loves you with perfectly patient, totally endless, grace-filled love. God loves you this way simply because you are God's kid.

2. God has decided that you are to spend all eternity in heaven—not because you have earned your place there, but because God has decided this and made that happen by the life, death, and resurrection of Jesus.

3. This is what Christmas and Easter are all about. Because God is love, God has done all that is necessary to ensure your eternal future.

4. Since you don't have that to worry about any longer, you can spend your time caring for yourself, your family, and your friends.

Chapter 33

The Teacher

Many people called Jesus "Teacher." Teaching is what he did all the time, responding to daily events in ways that taught people about the importance of loving God and each other. Often we saw displays of his divine wisdom and power. But for several important events during "Holy Week," Jesus did some obvious advanced planning because those particular events were too important to be left to chance. In both cases, he made secret arrangements with people he could trust and told them to be looking for discreet contacts from his disciples.

On Sunday, Jesus planned to teach a lesson about the value of humility and servanthood over might and power. The way he chose to do this was to parody the parade made by Governor Pilate when he rode into town on a warhorse followed by a well-armed military force. Jesus would instead ride into town on a farm animal—a donkey—followed by an unarmed group of people. To accomplish this, Jesus asked some friends to leave a young donkey on the street near their house and be ready when his disciples came to retrieve it. The disciples were instructed to untie the donkey, and they would know they had gotten the correct one if someone walked up to them and asked, "Why are you untying the donkey?" Jesus told them to answer with this counter-sign: "The Lord needs it and will send it back here shortly." The Palm Sunday parade was Jesus's way of teaching that he was the king referred to in Zechariah 9:9—"your king comes to you, righteous and victorious, lowly and riding on a donkey"—and that we were also to value the power of being a servant instead of what nations consider leadership and might.

The second time Jesus made similar arrangements in advance because of the extreme importance of the event was the night he celebrated the Passover meal with his disciples, packing it with a new and powerful meaning. This time, Jesus had arranged for a trusted friend in town to be carrying a water jar at a certain time. This was the man the disciples should follow without talking with him until he entered his house. At that point they were to give the verbal signal, "The Teacher asks, 'Where is my guest room where I may eat the Passover with my disciples?'" The man's response would be to show the disciples a room upstairs that had been readied for their dinner and where final preparations could be made by the disciples. Jesus used this meal to connect the giving of his life for us to the symbol of the salvation God had provided for his people in Egypt via the Passover Lamb.

This careful planning and the use of cloak-and-dagger code words teach us two important things. First, Holy Week was an extremely dangerous time for Jesus and the disciples to be in Jerusalem. Second, since careful and secretive plans were being made for Jesus's arrest and execution, Jesus needed to make careful and secretive plans for the important lessons he wanted to teach us during those days.

And the Teacher kept teaching—during his arrest, his trial, the mocking, crucifixion, death ... and resurrection!

Chapter 34

It Takes No Talent

When our son John was in the fifth grade, he made a decision to give up football and softball so he could concentrate on his new favorite sport: soccer. By the time he was in the seventh grade, he was playing on the junior varsity team of Rock Hill High School. He stuck with soccer all through high school after we moved to Boiling Springs. He made the varsity team as a sophomore.

But the coach John had in Rock Hill had a big influence on the boys because of his interesting philosophy. Some of the boys knew they were not as talented as some of the players they would be competing against, so the coach would repeat this statement at every practice: "It takes no talent to hustle and beat the other players to the ball."

He knew that by getting in shape so they could run hard for the entire game and be the first player to get to the ball, they would make opportunities for their team to win.

I've thought a lot about that coach's philosophy over the years and applied it to my life as I could. It takes no talent to show up where you are needed—like at someone's house in the time of an illness or a death with your loving presence. You don't even need to know what you should say. You just hustle to the place you need to be.

Just by faithfully showing up, you create opportunities to show God's love to others.

Chapter 35

Let's Go Back

In presidential elections, it seems that whichever party is out of power is the one calling us to look backwards to good old days in the past. It is an effective way to tug on our hearts, but the older I get, the less good I find in the old days.

I do not want to go back to the days of racial segregation that I remember so well from my childhood in the 1950s. I don't want to sit in the best seats at the movie theaters while Black children have to sit in the second-balcony "nosebleed section."

I don't want to go back to separate and not-so-equal schools, nor do I want to go back to separate bathrooms and water fountains for the different races. I don't want public swimming pools that only White people can swim in, and I would hate for it to be illegal for people to marry outside of their own race like it was until 1967.

I don't want to go back to the days when women were expected to be stay-at-home moms unless they were teachers or nurses and where only single women were allowed to be teachers. And I don't want to go back to the days when wives were expected to "love, honor, and obey" their husbands.

Chapter 36

Disaffiliation

Some United Methodist churches have decided to disaffiliate, but the good news is that others have decided to stay United Methodist. These congregations examined all the facts and came to the conclusion that the "facts" offered by the folks wanting to leave The United Methodist Church were overblown, often mistaken, and filled more with hyperbole than provable facts.

Perhaps they remembered that:

It didn't destroy our denomination when we started ordaining and appointing female clergy back in the 1950s.

It didn't destroy the church when we decided that divorce was forgivable—even for our clergy—back in the 1970s. (By the way, we had a bunch of former Baptist pastors join the UMC after they got divorced and were forced to leave their denomination.)

It didn't destroy the church—as many said it would—when we integrated our denomination back in the 1970s. Since then, Whites and Blacks and Asians have worshiped together under the UMC banner.

And we are stronger for removing all those barriers.

In recent years, we have even given more control of pastoral appointments to local churches. Back in the 1940s, pastors and churches found out on the same day—the last day of Annual Conference and just several days before "moving day"—where the bishop was assigning pastors, and there was no debate or consultation back then. In the words of my granddaughter's teachers, "You get what you get and you don't make a fit."

Judging by the fact that most of the churches that disaffiliated from the UMC last year decided not to join any other denomination but to remain independent, I'd say that it isn't the issue of LGBTQ that is driving the disaffiliation movement. Rather, it may be driven by folks who just want to be more like the Baptists with each church independent.

I hope folks who still have this decision to make will think calmly and prayerfully.

Conclusion

I wrote this tribute to my parents in September 2001 as I was clearing out my parents' home following my mother's death earlier that year. My father had died a decade earlier. The impact of these losses really hit me when I gave away our ping-pong table.

Dad didn't learn many new skills during his army service in World War II, but he did become a champion ping-pong player. He didn't hold the paddle like most folks; instead, he held it like a pencil with the paddle pointing down and the handle sticking up between his thumb and forefinger, which met on top of the paddle. With his other three fingers underneath the paddle, his grip enabled him to put unbelievable spins on the ball. Once it hit on his opponent's side, the ball would suddenly change its direction, and if you were lucky enough hit the ball, it would jump off your paddle in unpredictable directions. Many of my friends who thought they were good table tennis players were made to look pretty foolish by swinging at balls that jumped a foot or more from their expected positions. "Strike!" somebody would yell.

I got the ping-pong table for my birthday—either my thirteenth or fourteenth. It was just a three-quarter inch sheet of unfinished plywood that we had to paint green and then line in white. The white lines were fat and crooked, hardly a professional paint job. I meant to repaint it but never did. We put it on one side of the basement, thus putting an end to using the area for a roller-skating rink or anything else.

It took me a year of daily defeats before I learned how to return Dad's curves and win a game. My cousin John moved in with our family during his high school senior year, when his father was at Duke University being treated for cancer, and my cousin became my brother in the endless hours we spent in the basement playing ping-pong. Then there were other cousins who joined in the games. Some were second and third cousins; some were a lot older than I was, cousins I would never have gotten to know had it not been for that table.

Playing doubles was both fun and hazardous as we tried to return those curves while dodging my grandmother's old parked 1949 Plymouth, several foundation poles, and a collection of old bedsprings. My table was responsible for a ping-pong revival at my church, and youth gatherings there were not complete without a half hour of contests.

My father and I had a disagreement when I was nineteen—so sharp a disagreement that Mom thought it would be best if I moved into the dorm at Wofford College. Somehow I doubt we would have managed to reconcile without that table to bring us back together. We couldn't discuss our differences, but we could still slap ping-pong balls at each other. I seem to remember that winning became very important to both of us during this era.

As Dad got older and had trouble walking because of arthritis, a trip to the basement and a session of ping-pong would seem to peel decades off his age. At age seventy-five, he could still whip most of his opponents. I guess I haven't played more than ten games since Dad died in 1990. I just haven't wanted to.

Mom died in 2001, and the reality of her passing was reinforced by the rituals our culture uses to engrave the finality of death into our minds—the visitation, the funeral, the marked grave at the cemetery. At times, something will happen to remind me that my parents are dead, like the many times I've thought about picking up the phone to tell Mom about something funny that one of my kids said or did, and then I remember that there is nobody home anymore.

But the most profound moment occurred that day when the ping-pong table was carried out the basement door—that table that was marred and scarred by people who sometimes worked out their marred and scarred relationships on it. As I looked at the empty place it had occupied for four decades, I had the clearest reminder yet that death is the final disconnection in this life on earth.

There are no more ping-pong games to be played at my childhood home. The place where we connected is gone; so are my beloved parents.

About the Author

The Rev. Arthur H. Holt is a retired United Methodist pastor who grew up in Spartanburg, South Carolina, and is a 1972 graduate of Wofford College. He earned his Master of Divinity from Lutheran Theological Southern Seminary in 1979 and has pastored churches across South Carolina. Married to his wife, Penny, for more than fifty years, they have two children and four grandchildren.

www.ingramcontent.com/pod-product-compliance
Lightning Source LLC
Chambersburg PA
CBHW070203100426
42743CB00013B/3028